Soups Stews & Chilis

Publications International, Ltd.

Pictured on the front cover: Chicken Noodle Soup *(page 6)*.

Pictured on the back cover *(clockwise from top right):* Vegetarian Quinoa Chili *(page 172)*, Aromatic Asian Beef Stew *(page 70)* and Simmered Split Pea Soup *(page 16)*.

ISBN: 978-1-64558-735-4

Manufactured in China.

8 7 6 5 4 3 2 1

Microwave Cooking: Microwave ovens vary in wattage. Use the cooking times as guidelines and check for doneness before adding more time.

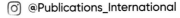

Let's get social!

@Publications_International

@PublicationsInternational

www.pilbooks.com

Contents

Classic Bowls

Chicken Noodle Soup

Makes 8 servings

2 tablespoons butter

1 cup chopped onion

1 cup sliced carrots

½ cup diced celery

2 tablespoons vegetable oil

1 pound chicken breast tenderloins

1 pound chicken thigh fillets

4 cups chicken broth, divided

2 cups water

1 tablespoon minced fresh parsley, plus additional for garnish

1½ teaspoons salt

½ teaspoon black pepper

3 cups uncooked egg noodles

1. Melt butter in large saucepan or Dutch oven over medium-low heat. Add onion, carrots and celery; cook 15 minutes or until vegetables are soft, stirring occasionally.

2. Meanwhile, heat oil in large skillet over medium-high heat. Add chicken in single layer; cook 12 minutes or until lightly browned and cooked through, turning once. Remove chicken to large cutting board. Add 1 cup broth to skillet; cook 1 minute, scraping up browned bits from bottom of skillet. Add broth to vegetables in saucepan. Stir in remaining 3 cups broth, water, 1 tablespoon parsley, salt and pepper.

3. Chop chicken into 1-inch pieces when cool enough to handle. Add to soup; bring to a boil over medium-high heat. Reduce heat to medium-low; cook 15 minutes. Add noodles; cook 15 minutes or until noodles are tender. Ladle into bowls; garnish with additional parsley.

Italian Wedding Soup

Makes 8 servings

Meatballs

- 2 eggs
- 2 cloves garlic, minced
- 1 teaspoon salt
- ⅛ teaspoon black pepper
- 1½ pounds meat loaf mix (ground beef and pork)
- ¾ cup plain dry bread crumbs
- ½ cup grated Parmesan cheese
- 2 tablespoons olive oil

Soup

- 1 onion, chopped
- 2 carrots, chopped
- 4 cloves garlic, minced
- 2 heads escarole or curly endive, coarsely chopped
- 8 cups chicken broth
- 1 can (about 14 ounces) Italian plum tomatoes, undrained, coarsely chopped
- 3 sprigs fresh thyme
- 1 teaspoon salt
- ½ teaspoon red pepper flakes
- 1 cup uncooked acini di pepe pasta

1. Whisk eggs, 2 cloves garlic, 1 teaspoon salt and black pepper in large bowl until blended. Stir in meat loaf mix, bread crumbs and cheese; mix gently until well blended. Shape mixture by tablespoonfuls into 1-inch balls.

2. Heat oil in large saucepan or Dutch oven over medium heat. Cook meatballs in batches 5 minutes or until browned. Remove to plate; set aside.

3. Add onion, carrots and 4 cloves garlic to saucepan; cook and stir 5 minutes or until onion is lightly browned. Add escarole; cook 2 minutes or until wilted. Stir in broth, tomatoes with juice, thyme, 1 teaspoon salt and red pepper flakes; bring to a boil over high heat. Reduce heat to medium-low; cook 15 minutes.

4. Add meatballs and pasta to soup; return to a boil over high heat. Reduce heat to medium; cook 10 minutes or until pasta is tender. Remove and discard thyme sprigs before serving.

Black Bean Soup

Makes 4 to 6 servings

2 tablespoons vegetable oil

1 cup diced onion

1 stalk celery, diced

2 carrots, diced

½ small green bell pepper, diced

4 cloves garlic, minced

4 cans (about 15 ounces each) black beans, rinsed and drained, divided

4 cups (32 ounces) chicken or vegetable broth, divided

2 tablespoons cider vinegar

2 teaspoons chili powder

½ teaspoon salt

½ teaspoon ground red pepper

½ teaspoon ground cumin

¼ teaspoon liquid smoke

Optional toppings: sour cream, chopped green onions and/or shredded Cheddar cheese

1. Heat oil in large saucepan or Dutch oven over medium-low heat. Add onion, celery, carrots, bell pepper and garlic; cook 10 minutes, stirring occasionally.

2. Combine half of beans and 1 cup broth in food processor or blender; process until smooth. Add to vegetables in saucepan.

3. Stir in remaining beans, 3 cups broth, vinegar, chili powder, salt, red pepper, cumin and liquid smoke; bring to a boil over high heat. Reduce heat to medium-low; cook 1 hour or until vegetables are tender and soup is thickened, stirring occasionally. Garnish as desired.

Baked Potato Soup

Makes 6 to 8 servings

3 medium russet potatoes (about 1 pound)

¼ cup (½ stick) butter

1 cup chopped onion

½ cup all-purpose flour

4 cups chicken or vegetable broth

1½ cups instant mashed potato flakes

1 cup water

1 cup half-and-half

1 teaspoon salt

½ teaspoon dried basil

½ teaspoon dried thyme

¼ teaspoon black pepper

1 cup (4 ounces) shredded Cheddar cheese

4 slices bacon, crisp-cooked and crumbled

1 green onion, chopped

1. Preheat oven to 400°F. Scrub potatoes and prick in several places with fork. Place in baking pan; bake 1 hour. Cool completely; peel and cut into ½-inch cubes. (Potatoes can be prepared several days in advance; refrigerate until ready to use.)

2. Melt butter in large saucepan or Dutch oven over medium heat. Add onion; cook and stir 3 minutes or until softened. Whisk in flour; cook and stir 1 minute. Gradually whisk in broth until well blended. Stir in mashed potato flakes, water, half-and-half, salt, basil, thyme and pepper; bring to a boil over medium-high heat. Reduce heat to medium; cook 5 minutes.

3. Stir in baked potato cubes; cook 10 to 15 minutes or until soup is thickened and heated through. Ladle into bowls; top with cheese, bacon and green onion.

Chicken Enchilada Soup

Makes 8 to 10 servings

2 tablespoons vegetable oil, divided

1½ pounds boneless skinless chicken breasts, cut into ½-inch pieces

½ cup chopped onion

2 cloves garlic, minced

2 cans (about 14 ounces each) chicken broth

3 cups water, divided

1 cup masa harina

1 package (16 ounces) pasteurized process cheese product, cubed

1 can (10 ounces) mild red enchilada sauce

1 teaspoon chili powder

½ teaspoon salt

½ teaspoon ground cumin

1 large tomato, seeded and chopped

Crispy tortilla strips*

If tortilla strips are not available, crumble tortilla chips into bite-size pieces.

1. Heat 1 tablespoon oil in large saucepan or Dutch oven over medium-high heat. Add chicken; cook and stir 10 minutes or until no longer pink. Transfer to medium bowl with slotted spoon; drain excess liquid from saucepan.

2. Heat remaining 1 tablespoon oil in same saucepan over medium-high heat. Add onion and garlic; cook and stir 3 minutes or until softened. Stir in broth.

3. Whisk 2 cups water into masa harina in large bowl until smooth. Whisk mixture into broth in saucepan. Stir in remaining 1 cup water, cheese product, enchilada sauce, chili powder, salt and cumin; bring to a boil over high heat. Add chicken. Reduce heat to medium-low; simmer 30 minutes, stirring frequently. Ladle soup into bowls; top with tomato and tortilla strips.

Classic French Onion Soup ▶

Makes 4 servings

¼ cup (½ stick) butter

3 large yellow onions, sliced

1 cup dry white wine

3 cans (about 14 ounces each) beef or chicken broth

1 teaspoon Worcestershire sauce

½ teaspoon salt

½ teaspoon dried thyme

4 slices French bread, toasted

1 cup (4 ounces) shredded Swiss cheese

Fresh thyme (optional)

Slow Cooker Directions

1. Melt butter in large skillet over medium heat. Add onions, cook and stir 15 minutes or until onions are soft and lightly browned. Stir in wine.

2. Combine onion mixture, broth, Worcestershire sauce, salt and dried thyme in slow cooker. Cover; cook on LOW 4 to 4½ hours.

3. Ladle soup into four bowls; top with bread slice and cheese. Broil 4 inches from heat 2 to 3 minutes or until cheese is bubbly and browned. Garnish with fresh thyme.

Simmered Split Pea Soup

Makes 6 servings

(pictured on page 4)

3 cans (about 14 ounces each) chicken broth

1 package (16 ounces) dried split peas, rinsed and sorted

1 onion, diced

2 carrots, diced

8 slices bacon, crisp-cooked and crumbled, divided

1 teaspoon black pepper

½ teaspoon dried thyme

1 bay leaf

Slow Cooker Directions

1. Combine broth, split peas, onion, carrots, half of bacon, pepper, thyme and bay leaf in slow cooker. Cover; cook on LOW 6 to 8 hours.

2. Remove and discard bay leaf. Adjust seasonings, if desired. Garnish with remaining bacon.

Classic Beef Stew

Makes 8 servings

2½ pounds cubed beef stew meat

2 tablespoons all-purpose flour

2 tablespoons olive oil

3 cups beef broth

16 baby carrots

8 fingerling potatoes, halved crosswise

1 medium onion, chopped

1 ounce dried oyster mushrooms, chopped

2 teaspoons garlic powder

1 teaspoon dried basil

1 teaspoon dried oregano

½ teaspoon dried rosemary

½ teaspoon dried marjoram

½ teaspoon dried sage

½ teaspoon dried thyme

Salt and black pepper

Chopped fresh Italian parsley (optional)

Slow Cooker Directions

1. Combine beef and flour in large resealable food storage bag; toss to coat. Heat 1 tablespoon oil in large skillet over medium-high heat. Add half of beef; cook and stir 4 minutes or until browned. Remove to slow cooker. Repeat with remaining oil and beef.

2. Add broth, carrots, potatoes, onion, mushrooms, garlic powder, basil, oregano, rosemary, marjoram, sage and thyme to slow cooker; stir to blend.

3. Cover; cook on LOW 10 to 12 hours or on HIGH 5 to 6 hours. Season with salt and pepper. Garnish with parsley.

Creamy Onion Soup ▶

Makes 4 servings

6 tablespoons (¾ stick) butter, divided

1 large sweet onion, thinly sliced (about 3 cups)

1 can (about 14 ounces) chicken broth

2 cubes chicken bouillon

¼ teaspoon black pepper

¼ cup all-purpose flour

1½ cups milk

1½ cups (6 ounces) shredded Colby-Jack cheese

Chopped fresh parsley (optional)

1. Melt 2 tablespoons butter in large saucepan or Dutch oven over medium heat. Add onion slices; cook 10 minutes or until soft and translucent, stirring occasionally. Add broth, bouillon and pepper; cook until bouillon is dissolved and mixture is heated through.

2. Meanwhile, melt remaining 4 tablespoons butter in medium saucepan. Whisk in flour; cook and stir 1 minute. Gradually whisk in milk until well blended. Cook 10 minutes or until very thick, stirring occasionally.

3. Add milk mixture to soup; cook over medium-low heat 5 to 10 minutes or until thickened, stirring occasionally. Add cheese; cook 5 minutes or until melted and smooth. Ladle into bowls; garnish with parsley.

Slow Cooker Chili Mac

Makes 6 servings

1 pound ground beef

½ cup chopped onion

1 can (about 14 ounces) diced tomatoes, drained

1 can (8 ounces) tomato sauce

2 tablespoons chili powder

1 teaspoon garlic salt

½ teaspoon ground cumin

¼ teaspoon red pepper flakes

¼ teaspoon black pepper

8 ounces uncooked elbow macaroni

Shredded Cheddar cheese (optional)

Slow Cooker Directions

1. Brown beef and onion in large skillet over medium heat 6 to 8 minutes, stirring to break up meat. Drain fat. Remove beef mixture to slow cooker.

2. Add tomatoes, tomato sauce, chili powder, garlic salt, cumin, red pepper flakes and black pepper; mix well. Cover; cook on LOW 4 hours.

3. Cook macaroni according to package directions until al dente; drain. Add macaroni to slow cooker; mix well. Cover; cook on LOW 1 hour. Garnish with cheese.

Curried Ginger Pumpkin Soup

Makes 8 servings

1 tablespoon vegetable oil

1 large sweet onion (such as Walla Walla), coarsely chopped

1 large Golden Delicious apple, peeled and coarsely chopped

3 (¼-inch) slices peeled fresh ginger

1½ teaspoons curry powder

2½ to 3 cups chicken broth, divided

2 cans (15 ounces each) solid-pack pumpkin

1 cup half-and-half

1 teaspoon salt

Black pepper

Roasted salted pumpkin seeds (optional)

1. Heat oil in large saucepan over medium heat. Add onion, apple, ginger and curry powder; cook and stir 10 minutes. Add ½ cup broth; cover and simmer 10 minutes or until apple is tender.

2. Pour onion mixture into blender; blend until smooth. Return to saucepan. (Or use hand-held immersion blender.)

3. Add pumpkin, 2 cups broth, half-and-half, salt and pepper; cook until heated through, stirring occasionally. If soup is too thick, add additional broth, a few tablespoons at a time, until soup reaches desired consistency. Sprinkle with pumpkin seeds, if desired.

Cincinnati Chili

Makes 4 servings

½ pound ground beef

1 cup diced onion

2 cans (8 ounces each) tomato sauce

1 can (about 15 ounces) kidney beans, rinsed and drained

1 cup water

2 teaspoons unsweetened cocoa powder

1½ teaspoons chili powder

¼ teaspoon ground cinnamon

¼ teaspoon salt (optional)

⅛ teaspoon black pepper

2 teaspoons cider vinegar

2 cups hot cooked whole wheat elbow macaroni* (cooked without fat or salt)

½ cup (2 ounces) shredded sharp Cheddar cheese (optional)

20 oyster crackers

If unavailable, may substitute with whole grain pasta shells.

1. Spray large skillet with nonstick cooking spray; heat over medium-high heat. Add beef and onion; cook and stir 6 to 8 minutes or until beef is browned. Drain fat.

2. Stir tomato sauce, beans, water, cocoa, chili powder, cinnamon, salt, if desired, pepper and vinegar into beef mixture in same skillet; cover and bring to a boil. Uncover, reduce heat to low; simmer 8 minutes or until slightly thickened and reduced to 4 cups. Stir occasionally. Spoon over macaroni; top with cheese, if desired, and crackers.

Note

Cincinnati chili (or "Cincinnati-style chili") is a regional style of chili that calls for uncommon ingredients such as cinnamon and cocoa. Oyster crackers sprinkled on top is also a characteristic of Cincinnati chili.

Minestrone Soup

Makes 4 to 6 servings

1 tablespoon olive oil

½ cup chopped onion

1 stalk celery, diced

1 carrot, diced

2 cloves garlic, minced

2 cups vegetable broth

1½ cups water

1 bay leaf

¾ teaspoon salt

½ teaspoon dried basil

½ teaspoon dried oregano

¼ teaspoon dried thyme

¼ teaspoon sugar

Ground black pepper

1 can (about 15 ounces) dark red kidney beans, rinsed and drained

1 can (about 15 ounces) navy beans or cannellini beans, rinsed and drained

1 can (about 14 ounces) diced tomatoes

1 cup diced zucchini (about 1 small)

½ cup uncooked small shell pasta

½ cup frozen cut green beans

¼ cup dry red wine

1 cup packed chopped fresh spinach

Grated Parmesan cheese (optional)

1. Heat oil in large saucepan or Dutch oven over medium-high heat. Add onion, celery, carrot and garlic; cook and stir 5 to 7 minutes or until vegetables are tender. Add broth, water, bay leaf, salt, basil, oregano, thyme, sugar and pepper; bring to a boil.

2. Stir in kidney beans, navy beans, tomatoes, zucchini, pasta, green beans and wine; cook 10 minutes, stirring occasionally.

3. Add spinach; cook 2 minutes or until pasta and zucchini are tender. Remove and discard bay leaf. Serve with cheese, if desired.

Chicken and Herb Stew

Makes 4 servings

½ cup all-purpose flour

½ teaspoon salt

¼ teaspoon black pepper

¼ teaspoon paprika

4 chicken drumsticks

4 chicken thighs

2 tablespoons olive oil

12 ounces unpeeled new red potatoes, quartered

2 carrots, quartered lengthwise, then cut crosswise into 3-inch pieces

1 green bell pepper, cut into thin strips

¾ cup chopped onion

2 cloves garlic, minced

1¾ cups water

¼ cup dry white wine

2 cubes chicken bouillon

1 tablespoon chopped fresh oregano

1 teaspoon chopped fresh rosemary leaves

2 tablespoons chopped fresh Italian parsley (optional)

1. Combine flour, salt, black pepper and paprika in shallow dish; stir until well blended. Coat chicken with flour mixture; shake off excess.

2. Heat oil in large skillet over medium-high heat. Add chicken; cook 10 minutes or until browned on both sides, turning once. Remove to plate.

3. Add potatoes, carrots, bell pepper, onion and garlic to skillet; cook 6 minutes or until vegetables are lightly browned, stirring occasionally. Add water, wine and bouillon; cook 1 minute, scraping up browned bits from bottom of skillet. Stir in oregano and rosemary.

4. Place chicken on top of vegetable mixture, turning several times to coat. Cover and simmer 45 to 50 minutes or until chicken is cooked through (165°F), turning occasionally. Garnish with parsley.

Butternut Squash Soup

Makes 4 servings

2   teaspoons olive oil

1   large sweet onion, chopped

1   medium red bell pepper, chopped

2   packages (10 ounces each) frozen puréed butternut squash, thawed

1   can (10¾ ounces) condensed chicken broth, undiluted

¼   teaspoon ground nutmeg

⅛   teaspoon white pepper

½   cup half-and-half

1. Heat oil in large saucepan over medium-high heat. Add onion and bell pepper; cook 5 minutes, stirring occasionally. Add squash, broth, nutmeg and white pepper; bring to a boil over high heat. Reduce heat to low; cover and simmer 15 minutes or until vegetables are very tender.

2. Purée soup in saucepan with hand-held immersion blender or in batches in food processor or blender. Return soup to saucepan.

3. Stir in half-and-half; heat through. Add additional half-and-half, if necessary, to thin soup to desired consistency.

Serving Suggestion

Garnish with a swirl of half-and-half or a sprinkling of fresh parsley.

Classic Chili

Makes 6 servings

1½ pounds ground beef

1½ cups chopped onion

1 cup chopped green bell pepper

2 cloves garlic, minced

3 cans (about 15 ounces each) dark red kidney beans, rinsed and drained

2 cans (about 15 ounces each) tomato sauce

1 can (about 14 ounces) diced tomatoes

2 to 3 teaspoons chili powder

1 to 2 teaspoons dry hot mustard

¾ teaspoon dried basil

½ teaspoon black pepper

1 to 2 dried hot chile peppers (optional)

Shredded Cheddar cheese (optional)

Fresh cilantro leaves (optional)

Slow Cooker Directions

1. Cook and stir beef, onion, bell pepper and garlic in large skillet over medium-high heat 6 to 8 minutes or until beef is browned and onion is tender. Drain fat. Remove to slow cooker.

2. Add beans, tomato sauce, diced tomatoes, chili powder, dry mustard, basil, black pepper and chile peppers, if desired, to slow cooker; mix well. Cover; cook on LOW 8 to 10 hours or on HIGH 4 to 5 hours. Remove and discard chile peppers before serving. Top with cheese, if desired. Garnish with cilantro.

Cream of Broccoli Soup with Croutons
Makes 8 servings

3 cups French or rustic bread, cut into ½-inch cubes

1 tablespoon butter, melted

1 tablespoon olive oil

¼ cup grated Parmesan cheese

2 tablespoons butter

1 large onion, chopped

8 cups (about 1½ pounds) chopped broccoli

3 cups chicken broth

1 cup whipping cream or half-and-half

1½ teaspoons salt

½ teaspoon black pepper

1. Preheat oven to 350°F. Combine bread cubes, 1 tablespoon melted butter and oil in large bowl; toss to coat. Add cheese; toss again. Spread bread cubes on 15×10-inch jelly-roll pan.

2. Bake 12 to 14 minutes or until golden brown, stirring after 8 minutes. Cool completely; remove to airtight container. (Croutons may be prepared up to 2 days before serving.)

3. Heat 2 tablespoons butter in large saucepan over medium heat. Add onion; cook 5 minutes, stirring occasionally. Add broccoli and broth; bring to a boil over high heat. Reduce heat to low; simmer 25 minutes or until broccoli is very tender. Cool 10 minutes.

4. Blend soup in blender or food processor until smooth. Return to saucepan; stir in cream, salt and pepper; cook over medium heat until heated through. (Do not boil.) Top with croutons.

Note

Soup may be cooled and refrigerated up to 2 days before serving.

Bean Lovers

Fasolada (Greek White Bean Soup)

Makes 4 to 6 servings

- 4 tablespoons olive oil, divided
- 1 large onion, diced
- 3 stalks celery, diced
- 3 carrots, diced
- 4 cloves garlic, minced
- ¼ cup tomato paste
- 1 teaspoon salt
- 1 teaspoon dried oregano
- ½ teaspoon ground cumin
- ¼ teaspoon black pepper
- 1 bay leaf
- 1 container (32 ounces) vegetable broth
- 3 cans (15 ounces each) cannellini beans, rinsed and drained
- 2 tablespoons lemon juice
- ¼ cup minced fresh parsley

1. Heat 2 tablespoons oil in large saucepan over medium-high heat. Add onion, celery and carrots; cook and stir 8 to 10 minutes or until vegetables are softened. Stir in garlic; cook and stir 30 seconds. Stir in tomato paste, salt, oregano, cumin, pepper and bay leaf; cook and stir 30 seconds.

2. Stir in broth; bring to a boil. Stir in beans; return to a boil. Reduce heat to medium-low; simmer 30 minutes. Stir in remaining 2 tablespoons oil and lemon juice. Remove and discard bay leaf. Sprinkle with parsley just before serving.

Sausage and Bean Stew

Makes 4 to 6 servings

2 cups fresh bread crumbs*

2 tablespoons olive oil, divided

1 pound uncooked pork sausage, cut into 2-inch pieces

1 leek, white and light green parts only, cut in half and thinly sliced

1 large onion, cut into quarters then cut into ¼-inch slices

1 teaspoon salt, divided

2 cloves garlic, minced

½ teaspoon dried thyme

½ teaspoon ground sage

¼ teaspoon paprika

¼ teaspoon ground allspice

¼ teaspoon black pepper

1 can (28 ounces) diced tomatoes

2 cans (about 15 ounces each) navy or cannellini beans, rinsed and drained

2 tablespoons whole grain mustard

Fresh thyme leaves (optional)

To make bread crumbs, cut 4 ounces stale baguette or country bread into several pieces; place in food processor. Pulse until coarse crumbs form.

1. Preheat oven to 350°F. Combine bread crumbs and 1 tablespoon oil in medium bowl; mix well.

2. Heat remaining 1 tablespoon oil in large ovenproof skillet over medium-high heat. Add sausage; cook 8 minutes or until browned, stirring occasionally. (Sausage will not be cooked through.) Remove to plate.

3. Add leek, onion and ½ teaspoon salt to skillet; cook 10 minutes or until vegetables are soft and beginning to brown, stirring occasionally. Add garlic; cook and stir 1 minute. Add dried thyme, sage, paprika, allspice and pepper; cook and stir 1 minute. Add tomatoes; cook 5 minutes, stirring occasionally. Stir in beans, mustard and remaining ½ teaspoon salt; bring to a simmer.

4. Return sausage to skillet, pushing down into bean mixture. Sprinkle with bread crumbs.

5. Bake 25 minutes or until bread crumbs are lightly browned and sausage is cooked through. Garnish with fresh thyme.

Black Bean and Bacon Soup ▶

Makes 6 to 8 servings

5 strips bacon, sliced

1 medium onion, diced

2 tablespoons ORTEGA® Fire-Roasted Diced Green Chiles

2 cans (15 ounces each) ORTEGA® Black Beans, undrained

4 cups chicken broth

½ cup ORTEGA® Taco Sauce, any variety

½ cup sour cream

4 ORTEGA® Yellow Corn Taco Shells, crumbled

COOK bacon in large pot over medium heat 5 minutes or until crisp. Add onion and chiles. Cook 5 minutes or until onion begins to brown. Stir in beans, broth and taco sauce. Bring to a boil. Reduce heat to low. Simmer 20 minutes.

PURÉE half of soup in food processor until smooth (or use immersion blender in pot). Return puréed soup to pot and stir to combine. Serve with dollop of sour cream and crumbled taco shells.

Note

For a less chunky soup, purée the entire batch and cook an additional 15 minutes.

Salsa Verde Chicken Stew

Makes 4 to 6 servings

(pictured on page 36)

1 tablespoon vegetable oil

1½ pounds boneless skinless chicken breasts, cut into ¾-inch pieces

2 cans (about 15 ounces each) black beans, rinsed and drained

1 jar (24 ounces) salsa verde

1½ cups frozen corn

¾ cup chopped fresh cilantro

Optional toppings: sour cream, tortilla chips and/or diced avocado

1. Heat oil in large saucepan over medium-high heat. Add chicken; cook and stir 5 minutes or until chicken begins to brown.

2. Stir in beans and salsa; bring to a simmer. Reduce heat to low; cover and cook 8 minutes.

3. Stir in corn; cook, uncovered, 3 minutes or until heated through. Remove from heat; stir in cilantro. Top as desired.

Baked Bean Stew

Makes 8 servings

1 cup chopped onion

1 cup chopped green pepper

1 tablespoon vegetable oil

12 ounces boneless skinless chicken breast or tenders, cut into ½-inch pieces

2 cans (15 ounces each) baked beans or pork and beans

1 can (15 ounces) garbanzo beans or black-eyes or 1½ cups cooked dry-packaged garbanzo beans or black-eyes, rinsed, drained

1 can (14½ ounces) diced tomatoes with roasted garlic, undrained

¾ teaspoon dried sage leaves

½ teaspoon ground cumin

Salt and pepper, to taste

1. Cook onion and green pepper in oil in large saucepan until tender, 3 to 4 minutes. Add chicken and cook over medium heat until browned, 3 to 4 minutes.

2. Add beans, tomatoes, and herbs to saucepan; heat to boiling. Reduce heat and simmer, uncovered, 8 to 10 minutes. Season to taste with salt and pepper.

Tip

Frozen chopped onion and green pepper can be used. Stew can be prepared 1 to 2 days in advance; refrigerate, covered. Stew can also be frozen up to 2 months.

US Dry Bean Board

Country Bean Soup

Makes 6 servings

1¼ cups dried navy beans or lima beans, rinsed and sorted

2½ cups water

4 ounces ham or salt pork, chopped

¼ cup chopped onion

½ teaspoon dried oregano

¼ teaspoon salt

¼ teaspoon ground ginger

¼ teaspoon dried sage

¼ teaspoon black pepper

2 cups milk

2 tablespoons butter

1. Place beans in large saucepan; add water to cover. Bring to a boil over medium-high heat. Reduce heat to medium-low; simmer 2 minutes. Remove from heat; cover and let stand 1 hour.

2. Drain beans and return to saucepan. Stir in 2½ cups water, ham, onion, oregano, salt, ginger, sage and pepper. Bring to a boil over high heat. Reduce heat to medium-low; cover and simmer 2 hours or until beans are tender. (If necessary, add additional water to keep beans covered during cooking.)

3. Add milk and butter; cook and stir until heated through.

Red Bean Soup

Makes 6 servings

- 1 pound dried red kidney beans
- 1 sprig fresh thyme, plus additional for garnish
- 1 sprig fresh parsley
- 2 tablespoons butter
- 1 onion, finely chopped
- 4 carrots, chopped
- 2 stalks celery, chopped
- 2½ quarts water, divided
- 1 pound smoked ham hocks
- 3 cloves garlic, finely chopped
- 1 bay leaf
- ½ teaspoon salt
- ¼ teaspoon black pepper
- 2 tablespoons fresh lemon juice
- Sour cream (optional)

1. Soak beans in 1 quart water in large bowl 6 hours or overnight. Drain and rinse beans. Tie together thyme and parsley sprigs with kitchen string.

2. Melt butter in large saucepan or Dutch oven over medium-high heat. Add onion; cook and stir 3 minutes or until softened. Add carrots and celery; cook and stir 5 minutes or until beginning to brown. Add remaining 1½ quarts water, beans, ham hocks, garlic, bay leaf and reserved thyme and parsley sprigs; bring to a boil over high heat. Reduce heat to low; cover and simmer 1 hour 30 minutes or until beans are softened. Remove and discard bones, thyme and parsley sprigs and bay leaf. Stir in salt and pepper.

3. Process soup in batches in food processor or blender until smooth. Return to saucepan; bring to a simmer. Stir in lemon juice and season with additional salt and pepper. Serve with sour cream, if desired; garnish with additional thyme.

Black Bean Soup

Substitute dried black beans for the red kidney beans. Proceed as directed, simmering soup 1½ to 2 hours or until beans are tender. Add 4 to 5 tablespoons dry sherry, to taste, just before serving.

Cranberry Bean Soup

Substitute dried cranberry beans for the red kidney beans. Proceed as directed, simmering soup 2 to 2¼ hours or until beans are tender. (Cranberry beans can be found in specialty food stores. They are the color of cranberries but taste similar to kidney beans.)

Savory Bean Stew

Makes 6 servings

1 cup frozen vegetable blend (onions, celery, red and green bell peppers)

1 can (about 15 ounces) chickpeas, rinsed and drained

1 can (about 15 ounces) pinto beans, rinsed and drained

1 can (about 15 ounces) black beans, rinsed and drained

1 can (about 14 ounces) diced tomatoes with roasted garlic, undrained

¾ teaspoon dried thyme

¾ teaspoon dried sage

½ to ¾ teaspoon dried oregano

1 tablespoon all-purpose flour

¾ cup vegetable broth, divided

Polenta

3 cups water

¾ cup yellow cornmeal

¾ teaspoon salt, plus additional for seasoning

Black pepper

Slow Cooker Directions

1. Combine vegetable blend, chickpeas, beans, tomatoes with juice, thyme, sage and oregano in slow cooker. Stir flour into ½ cup broth in small bowl; whisk into bean mixture. Cover; cook on LOW 4 hours or until vegetables are tender and juice is thickened.

2. Meanwhile, prepare polenta. Bring 3 cups water to a boil in large saucepan. Reduce heat to low; gradually stir in cornmeal and ¾ teaspoon salt. Cook 15 minutes or until cornmeal thickens. Season to taste with additional salt and pepper. Keep warm.

3. Stir remaining ¼ cup broth into slow cooker. Spread polenta on plate; top with stew.

Black Bean Chili

Makes 6 servings

1 pound dried black beans, rinsed and sorted

Cold water

6 cups water

1 bay leaf

3 tablespoons vegetable oil

2 large onions, chopped

3 cloves garlic, minced

1 can (about 14 ounces) diced tomatoes

2 to 3 fresh jalapeño peppers, stemmed, seeded and minced

2 tablespoons chili powder

1½ teaspoons salt

1 teaspoon paprika

1 teaspoon dried oregano

1 teaspoon unsweetened cocoa powder

½ teaspoon ground cumin

¼ teaspoon ground cinnamon

1 tablespoon red wine vinegar

6 mini sourdough bread loaves (optional)

Optional toppings: plain yogurt or sour cream, picante sauce, sliced green onions and/or chopped fresh cilantro

1. Place beans in 8-quart Dutch oven. Add enough cold water to cover beans by 2 inches. Cover; bring to a boil over high heat. Boil 2 minutes. Remove from heat; let soak, covered, 1 hour. Drain.

2. Add 6 cups water and bay leaf to beans in Dutch oven. Return to heat. Bring to a boil. Reduce heat and simmer, partially covered, 1 to 2 hours or until tender.

3. Heat oil in large skillet over medium heat. Add onions and garlic; cook 6 to 8 minutes until onions are tender. Coarsely chop tomatoes; add to skillet. Add jalapeño peppers, chili powder, salt, paprika, oregano, cocoa, cumin and cinnamon. Simmer 15 minutes. Add tomato mixture to beans. Stir in vinegar; simmer 30 minutes or until beans are very tender and chili has thickened slightly. Remove and discard bay leaf. Ladle chili into bread bowls, if desired, or individual bowls. Top as desired.

Northwoods Smoked Ham and Bean Soup

Makes 6 to 8 servings

2 tablespoons olive oil

2 large onions, chopped

6 cloves garlic, minced

6 cups chicken broth

2 smoked ham hocks

2 cups cubed cooked smoked ham

1 can (28 ounces) whole plum tomatoes, drained and coarsely chopped

1 bunch fresh parsley, stemmed and chopped

4 sprigs fresh thyme

4 bay leaves

2 cans (about 15 ounces each) cannellini beans, rinsed and drained

½ pound cooked orecchiette, cavatelli or ditalini pasta

Salt and black pepper

Slow Cooker Directions

1. Heat oil in large skillet over medium heat. Add onions; cook 10 minutes or until soft and fragrant, stirring occasionally. Add garlic; cook 1 minute.

2. Place onion and garlic mixture, broth, ham hocks, ham, tomatoes, parsley, thyme and bay leaves in **CROCK-POT®** slow cooker. Cook on LOW 10 hours or on HIGH 6 hours.

3. Stir in beans and pasta. Cover; cook on HIGH 10 minutes or until heated through. Remove and discard bay leaves. Season with salt and pepper.

Souper Pastry Bowls

Makes 2 servings

½ of a 17.3-ounce package
PEPPERIDGE FARM®
Frozen Puff Pastry Sheets
(1 sheet)

1 egg

1 tablespoon water

Assorted fresh herb leaves
(rosemary, thyme or sage)
(optional)

1 can (18.6 to 19 ounces)
CAMPBELL'S® Chunky™
Soup or Chili, any variety

1. Thaw the pastry sheet at room temperature for 40 minutes or until it's easy to handle. Heat the oven to 400°F. Stir the egg and water.

2. Unfold the pastry sheet on a lightly floured surface. Cut in half. Roll each half into a 9×9-inch square. Press the pastry into **2** oven-safe bowls (16-ounces **each**), fold over the corners to make a rim. Press the herb leaves into the pastry, if desired. Brush lightly with the egg mixture.

3. Bake for 20 minutes or until golden. Let cool on a wire rack for 5 minutes.

4. Heat the soup or chili according to the package directions.

5. Remove the pastry from the bowls and place on 2 serving plates or bowls. Using a small knife, cut a slit into center and push down to form a bowl. Divide the soup between the pastry bowls. Serve immediately.

Campbell's Kitchen Tip

For a quicker version, bake 1 package (10 ounces) PEPPERIDGE FARM® Frozen Puff Pastry Shells according to package directions. Heat the soup or chili according to the package directions. Place the shells on serving plates or bowls, push in the pastry centers and divide the soup among the shells.

Fresh Tomato Chili

Makes 4 servings

- 1 tablespoon olive oil
- 1 small onion, chopped (about 1 cup)
- 1 clove garlic, minced
- 1 medium tomato, diced (about 1½ cups)
- 1 cup frozen corn
- 1 cup canned kidney beans, rinsed and drained
- 1 can (8 ounces) tomato sauce
- ½ to ⅔ cup vegetable broth, divided
- 1 teaspoon chili powder
- ½ teaspoon ground cumin
- ¼ teaspoon dried oregano
- ⅛ teaspoon salt
- ⅛ teaspoon black pepper
- ⅛ teaspoon red pepper flakes
- 1 cup water
- 1 cup uncooked instant brown rice

1. Heat oil in large nonstick skillet or saucepan over medium-high heat. Add onion and garlic; cook and stir 5 minutes. Add tomato and corn; cook and stir 2 minutes.

2. Add beans, tomato sauce, ½ cup broth, chili powder, cumin, oregano, salt, black pepper and red pepper flakes. Simmer 6 to 8 minutes. Add remaining broth if chili is too thick.

3. Meanwhile, bring water to a boil in small saucepan. Reduce heat to low. Add rice; cover and simmer 5 minutes. Remove from heat; let stand 5 minutes. Fluff with fork. Serve chili over rice.

Mediterranean Eggplant and White Bean Stew

Makes 6 servings

1	tablespoon olive oil
1	medium onion, chopped
1	medium eggplant (1 pound), peeled and cut into ¾-inch pieces
4	cloves garlic, minced
1	can (28 ounces) stewed tomatoes, undrained
2	bell peppers (1 red and 1 yellow), cut into ¾-inch chunks
1	teaspoon dried oregano
¼	teaspoon red pepper flakes (optional)
1	can (about 15 ounces) Great Northern or cannellini beans, rinsed and drained
6	tablespoons grated Parmesan cheese
¼	cup chopped fresh basil

1. Heat oil in large saucepan over medium heat. Add onion; cook and stir 5 minutes. Add eggplant and garlic; cook and stir 5 minutes. Stir in tomatoes with juice, bell peppers, oregano and red pepper flakes, if desired. Reduce heat to medium-low; cover and simmer 20 minutes or until vegetables are tender.

2. Stir in beans; simmer, uncovered, 5 minutes. Ladle into shallow bowls; top with cheese and basil.

Chorizo and Black Bean Chili

Makes 6 to 8 servings

1 tablespoon vegetable oil

1 cup diced onion

½ cup diced green bell pepper

1 pound chorizo sausage, casings removed

1 packet (1.25 ounces) ORTEGA® Reduced Sodium Chili Seasoning Mix

2 cups water

1 jar (16 ounces) ORTEGA® Black Bean and Corn Salsa

1 can (15 ounces) ORTEGA® Black Beans, rinsed, drained

6 to 8 ORTEGA® Yellow Corn Taco Shells, broken (optional)

HEAT oil over medium-high heat in large saucepan. Add onion and bell pepper; cook and stir 4 minutes or until slightly softened.

STIR in chorizo. Sprinkle seasoning mix over chorizo; stir to coat evenly. Stir in water, salsa and beans.

BRING to a boil. Reduce heat to medium-low; simmer 30 minutes.

TOP each serving with taco shells, if desired.

Tex-Mex Black Bean and Corn Stew

Makes 4 servings

1 tablespoon canola or vegetable oil

1 small onion, chopped

4 cloves garlic, minced

1 teaspoon chili powder

1 teaspoon ground cumin

1 can (about 14 ounces) fire-roasted diced tomatoes

¾ cup salsa

2 medium zucchini or yellow squash (or 1 of each), cut into ½-inch pieces

1 can (about 15 ounces) black beans, rinsed and drained

1 cup frozen corn

½ cup (2 ounces) shredded Cheddar or pepper jack cheese

¼ cup chopped fresh cilantro or green onion

1. Heat oil in large saucepan over medium heat. Add onion; cook and stir 5 minutes. Add garlic, chili powder and cumin; cook and stir 1 minute.

2. Stir in tomatoes, salsa, zucchini, beans and corn; bring to a boil over high heat. Reduce heat to low; cover and simmer 20 minutes or until vegetables are tender. Ladle into shallow bowls; top with cheese and cilantro.

Global Flavors

Chilled Avocado Soup

Makes 4 to 6 servings

4 ripe avocados

1 cup chicken broth

¾ cup sour cream

3 green onions, chopped

2 tablespoons ORTEGA® Taco Sauce, hot

1 jar (8 ounces) ORTEGA® Green Taco Sauce

2 cups water

Juice of 1 lime

½ teaspoon salt

Additional ORTEGA® Green Taco Sauce (optional)

ORTEGA® Tostada Shells, broken in half (optional)

CUT avocados in half and remove pits. Scrape avocado flesh into food processor or blender.

ADD broth, sour cream, green onions and 2 tablespoons taco sauce. Process using on/off pulsing action until ingredients are finely chopped.

ADD 1 jar taco sauce, water,* lime juice and salt. Pulse until evenly mixed, stopping occasionally to scrape sides of bowl with rubber spatula. Process 2 minutes or until smooth. Refrigerate at least 2 hours or until chilled before serving.

GARNISH with 1 tablespoon additional taco sauce and serve with tostada shells, if desired.

Pour some of the water into the emptied jar and shake to release any trapped sauce; add to food processor.

Tip

To remove pits from avocados without leaving behind a lot of the meat, cut the avocados in half lengthwise, and twist to separate the halves. Carefully stab the center of the pit with the edge of a paring knife blade, then twist slightly; the pit should come out easily.

Aromatic Asian Beef Stew

Makes 6 to 8 servings

 4 tablespoons vegetable oil, divided

 3 pounds beef for stew, cut into 1¼-inch pieces

12 shallots, peeled

 2 medium onions, chopped

 4 cloves garlic, minced

 3 cups water

 2 tablespoons sugar

1½ teaspoons salt

 1 teaspoon anise seeds

 ¼ teaspoon ground cinnamon

 ¼ teaspoon black pepper

 2 bay leaves

 1 pound white turnips (3 or 4) *or* 1 icicle radish or Japanese daikon, peeled and cut into wedges

 1 pound carrots, cut into 1½-inch pieces

 3 (2×½-inch) strips lemon peel

 1 can (6 ounces) tomato paste

   Japanese daikon sprouts tied together with green onion top (optional)

1. Heat large wok over medium-high heat. Drizzle 1 tablespoon oil into wok. Add half of beef; stir-fry 5 minutes or until browned. Remove to large bowl. Repeat with 1 tablespoon oil and remaining beef. Remove beef; set aside.

2. Heat 1 tablespoon oil in wok. Add shallots; stir-fry until browned. Remove to small bowl. Heat remaining 1 tablespoon oil in wok. Add onions and garlic; stir-fry 2 minutes.

3. Return beef and all juices to wok. Add water, sugar and seasonings. Cover; bring to a boil. Reduce heat to low; simmer 1¼ hours or until meat is almost tender.

4. Add turnips, carrots, shallots and lemon peel to beef. Cover; cook 30 minutes or until meat is tender, stirring occasionally. Remove and discard bay leaves and lemon peel. Stir tomato paste into stew; cook and stir until sauce boils and thickens. Remove to serving bowl. Garnish with diakon sprouts, if desired.

Simmering Hot & Sour Soup

Makes 4 servings

2 cans (about 14 ounces each) chicken broth

1 cup chopped cooked chicken or pork

4 ounces shiitake mushroom caps, thinly sliced

½ cup sliced bamboo shoots, cut into thin strips

3 tablespoons rice wine vinegar

2 tablespoons soy sauce

1½ teaspoons Chinese chili paste *or* 1 teaspoon hot chili oil

4 ounces firm tofu, drained and cut into ½-inch pieces

2 teaspoons dark sesame oil

2 tablespoons cornstarch

2 tablespoons cold water

Chopped fresh cilantro or sliced green onions (optional)

Slow Cooker Directions

1. Combine broth, chicken, mushrooms, bamboo shoots, vinegar, soy sauce and chili paste in slow cooker. Cover; cook on LOW 3 to 4 hours.

2. Stir in tofu and sesame oil. Blend cornstarch and water in small bowl until smooth. Stir into slow cooker. Turn slow cooker to HIGH. Cover; cook on HIGH 15 minutes or until soup is thickened. Garnish with cilantro.

French Lentil Soup ▶

Makes 4 to 6 servings

3 tablespoons olive oil

1 medium onion, chopped

1 carrot, chopped

1 stalk celery, chopped

1 clove garlic, minced

8 ounces dried lentils, rinsed and sorted

3 cups chicken broth

1 can (about 14 ounces) stewed tomatoes

½ cup cola

Salt and black pepper

½ cup grated Parmesan cheese (optional)

1. Heat oil in large skillet over medium heat. Add onion, carrot, celery and garlic; cook 8 minutes or until vegetables are tender but not browned, stirring occasionally.

2. Stir in lentils, broth, tomatoes and cola; bring to a boil over high heat. Reduce heat to low; cover and simmer 30 minutes or until lentils are tender.

3. Season with salt and pepper; sprinkle with Parmesan, if desired.

Tortilla Soup

Makes 4 servings

(pictured on page 66)

Vegetable oil

3 (6- or 7-inch) corn tortillas, halved and cut into strips

½ cup chopped onion

1 clove garlic, minced

2 cans (about 14 ounces each) chicken broth

1 can (about 14 ounces) diced tomatoes

1 cup shredded cooked chicken

2 teaspoons fresh lime juice

1 small avocado, diced

2 tablespoons chopped fresh cilantro

1. Pour oil to depth of ½ inch in small skillet. Heat over medium-high heat until oil reaches 360°F on deep-fry thermometer. Add tortilla strips, a few at a time; fry 1 minute or until crisp and lightly browned. Remove with slotted spoon; drain on paper towels.

2. Heat 2 teaspoons oil in large saucepan over medium heat. Add onion and garlic; cook and stir 6 to 8 minutes or until onion is softened. Add broth and tomatoes; bring to a boil. Cover; reduce heat to low. Simmer 15 minutes.

3. Add chicken and lime juice; simmer 5 minutes. Top soup with tortilla strips, avocado and cilantro.

Chili Verde

Makes 4 servings

½ to ¾ pound boneless lean pork, cut into 1-inch cubes

1 large onion, halved and thinly sliced

6 cloves garlic, chopped or sliced

½ cup water

1 pound fresh tomatillos

1 can (about 14 ounces) chicken broth

1 can (4 ounces) diced mild green chiles, drained

1 teaspoon ground cumin

1½ cups cooked navy or Great Northern beans *or* 1 can (about 15 ounces) Great Northern beans, rinsed and drained

½ cup lightly packed fresh cilantro, chopped

Jalapeño peppers, sliced (optional)

1. Place pork, onion, garlic and water in large saucepan. Cover; simmer over medium-low heat 30 minutes, stirring occasionally (add more water if necessary). Uncover; boil over medium-high heat until liquid is evaporated and meat is browned.

2. Stir in tomatillos and broth. Cover; simmer over medium heat 20 minutes or until tomatillos are tender. Pull tomatillos apart with two forks. Add chiles and cumin.

3. Cover; simmer over medium-low heat 45 minutes or until meat is tender and pulls apart easily. (Add more water or broth, if necessary, to keep liquid at same level.) Add beans; simmer 10 minutes or until heated through. Stir in cilantro. Top with jalapeño peppers, if desired.

Shantung Twin Mushroom Soup

Makes 6 servings

- 1 package (1 ounce) dried shiitake mushrooms
- 2 teaspoons vegetable oil
- 1 large onion, coarsely chopped
- 2 cloves garlic, minced
- 2 cups sliced button mushrooms
- 2 cans (about 14 ounces each) chicken broth
- 2 ounces cooked ham, cut into thin slivers
- ½ cup thinly sliced green onions
- 1 tablespoon dry sherry
- 1 tablespoon reduced-sodium soy sauce
- 1 tablespoon cornstarch

1. Place shiitake mushrooms in small bowl; cover with boiling water. Let stand 20 minutes to soften. Rinse well. Drain mushrooms; squeeze out excess water. Cut off and discard stems; slice caps.

2. Heat oil in large saucepan over medium heat. Add onion and garlic; cook and stir 1 minute. Stir in shiitake and button mushrooms; cook 4 minutes, stirring occasionally.

3. Stir in broth; bring to a boil over high heat. Reduce heat to medium; cover and simmer 15 minutes.

4. Stir in ham and green onions; cook until heated through. Stir sherry and soy sauce into cornstarch in small bowl until smooth. Add to soup; cook 2 minutes or until thickened, stirring occasionally.

North African Chicken Soup

Makes 4 servings

¾ teaspoon paprika

½ teaspoon ground ginger

½ teaspoon ground cumin

½ teaspoon ground allspice

8 ounces boneless skinless chicken breasts, cut into 1-inch pieces

2½ cups chicken broth

2 cups peeled sweet potato, cut into ½-inch pieces

1 cup chopped onion

½ cup water

3 cloves garlic, minced

1 teaspoon sugar

2 cups undrained canned tomatoes, cut up

Black pepper

1. Combine paprika, ginger, cumin and allspice in small bowl; mix well. Combine 1 teaspoon spice mixture and chicken in medium bowl; toss to coat.

2. Spray large saucepan with nonstick cooking spray; heat over medium-high heat. Add chicken; cook and stir 3 to 4 minutes or until chicken is cooked through. Remove to plate.

3. Combine broth, sweet potato, onion, water, garlic, sugar and remaining spice mixture in same saucepan; bring to a boil over high heat. Reduce heat to medium-low; simmer, covered, 10 minutes or until sweet potato is tender. Stir in tomatoes and chicken; heat through. Season to taste with pepper.

Chili á la Mexico

Makes 6 servings

2 pounds ground beef

2 cups finely chopped onions

2 cloves garlic, minced

1 can (28 ounces) whole tomatoes, undrained and coarsely chopped

1 can (6 ounces) tomato paste

1½ to 2 tablespoons chili powder

1 teaspoon ground cumin

¼ teaspoon salt

¼ teaspoon ground red pepper

¼ teaspoon ground cloves (optional)

Lime wedges and sprigs fresh cilantro (optional)

1. Brown beef in deep skillet over medium-high heat 6 to 8 minutes, stirring to break up meat. Drain fat. Add onions and garlic; cook and stir 5 minutes or until onions are softened.

2. Stir in tomatoes with juice, tomato paste, chili powder, cumin, salt, ground red pepper and cloves, if desired. Bring to a boil over high heat. Reduce heat to low; cover and simmer 30 minutes, stirring occasionally. Ladle into bowls. Garnish with lime and cilantro, if desired.

Middle Eastern Chicken Soup

Makes 4 servings

- 1 can (about 14 ounces) chicken broth
- 1 can (about 15 ounces) chickpeas, rinsed and drained
- 1 cup chopped cooked chicken
- 1 small onion, chopped
- 1 carrot, chopped
- 1 clove garlic, minced
- 1 teaspoon dried oregano
- 1 teaspoon ground cumin
- ½ (10-ounce) package fresh spinach, stemmed and coarsely chopped
- ⅛ teaspoon black pepper

1. Combine broth, 1½ cans water, chickpeas, chicken, onion, carrot, garlic, oregano and cumin in medium saucepan. Bring to a boil over high heat. Reduce heat to medium-low; cover and simmer 15 minutes.

2. Stir in spinach and pepper; simmer, uncovered, 2 minutes or until spinach is wilted.

West African Chicken Stew

Makes 6 servings

½ cup all-purpose flour

2 teaspoons pumpkin pie spice

1 teaspoon paprika

½ teaspoon cracked black pepper

6 bone-in chicken thighs

6 chicken drumsticks

2 tablespoons vegetable oil

1 can (10¾ ounces) CAMPBELL'S® Condensed French Onion Soup

½ cup water

1 cup raisins*

½ cup orange juice

1 teaspoon grated orange zest

2 tablespoons chopped fresh parsley or cilantro leaves

6 cups hot cooked couscous

You may substitute chopped prunes or apricots for the raisins, if you like.

Slow Cooker Directions

1. Mix the flour, pumpkin pie spice, paprika and black pepper on a plate. Coat the chicken with the flour mixture.

2. Heat the oil in a 12-inch skillet over medium heat. Add the chicken and cook for 10 minutes or until well browned.

3. Stir the soup, water, raisins, orange juice and orange zest in a 6-quart slow cooker. Add the chicken and turn to coat.

4. Cover and cook on LOW for 7 to 8 hours** or until the chicken is cooked through.

5. Stir the parsley into the cooker. Serve with the couscous.

Or on HIGH for 4 to 5 hours.

Chile Verde Chicken Stew

Makes 6 servings

⅓ cup all-purpose flour

1½ teaspoons salt, divided

¼ teaspoon black pepper

1½ pounds boneless skinless chicken breasts, cut into 1½-inch pieces

4 tablespoons vegetable oil, divided

1 pound tomatillos (about 9), husked and halved

2 onions, chopped

2 cans (4 ounces each) diced mild green chiles

1 tablespoon dried oregano

1 tablespoon ground cumin

2 cloves garlic, chopped

1 teaspoon sugar

2 cups reduced-sodium chicken broth

8 ounces Mexican beer

5 unpeeled red potatoes, diced

Optional toppings: chopped fresh cilantro, sour cream, shredded Monterey Jack cheese, lime wedges, diced avocado and/or hot pepper sauce

1. Combine flour, 1 teaspoon salt and pepper in large bowl. Add chicken; toss to coat. Heat 2 tablespoons oil in large nonstick skillet over medium heat. Add chicken; cook until lightly browned on all sides, stirring occasionally. Transfer to Dutch oven.

2. Heat remaining 2 tablespoons oil in same skillet. Stir in tomatillos, onions, chiles, oregano, cumin, garlic, sugar and remaining ½ teaspoon salt. Cook and stir 20 minutes or until vegetables are softened. Stir in broth and beer. Working in batches, process mixture in food processor or blender until almost smooth.

3. Add mixture to chicken in Dutch oven. Stir in potatoes. Cover; bring to a boil over medium-high heat. Reduce heat to low; simmer 1 hour or until potatoes are tender, stirring occasionally. Top as desired.

Variation

Omit potato and serve over hot white rice.

Jamaican Black Bean Stew

Makes 8 servings

2 cups uncooked brown rice

2 pounds sweet potatoes

3 pounds butternut squash

1 can (about 14 ounces) vegetable broth

1 large onion, coarsely chopped

3 cloves garlic, minced

1 tablespoon curry powder

1½ teaspoons ground allspice

½ teaspoon ground red pepper

¼ teaspoon salt

2 cans (15 ounces each) black beans, rinsed and drained

½ cup raisins

3 tablespoons fresh lime juice

1 cup diced tomato

1 cup diced peeled cucumber

1. Prepare rice according to package directions. Meanwhile, peel sweet potatoes; cut into ¾-inch pieces to measure 4 cups. Peel squash; remove seeds. Cut into ¾-inch cubes to measure 5 cups.

2. Combine sweet potatoes, squash, broth, onion, garlic, curry powder, allspice, red pepper and salt in Dutch oven; bring to a boil over high heat. Reduce heat to low; cover and simmer 15 minutes or until sweet potatoes and squash are tender. Add beans and raisins; simmer 5 minutes or until heated through. Stir in lime juice.

3. Serve stew over brown rice; top with tomato and cucumber.

Portuguese Potato and Greens Soup ▶

Makes 4 servings

2 tablespoons olive oil

1 cup chopped onion

1 cup chopped carrots

2 cloves garlic, minced

1 pound unpeeled new red potatoes, cut into 1-inch pieces

2 cups water

1 can (about 14 ounces) chicken broth

8 ounces chorizo sausage, casings removed

8 ounces kale

   Salt and black pepper

1. Heat oil in large saucepan over medium heat. Add onion, carrots and garlic; cook and stir 5 to 6 minutes or until lightly browned. Add potatoes, water and broth. Bring to a boil. Reduce heat to low; cover and simmer 10 to 15 minutes or until potatoes are tender.

2. Meanwhile, heat large nonstick skillet over medium heat. Crumble chorizo into skillet; cook and stir 5 to 6 minutes or until sausage is cooked through. Drain on paper towel-lined plate.

3. Wash kale; remove tough stems. Cut into thin slices.

4. Add sausage and kale to broth mixture; cook over medium heat 4 to 5 minutes or until heated through. (Kale should be bright green and slightly crunchy.) Season with salt and pepper.

Mediterranean Chili

Makes 5 servings

1 tablespoon olive oil

½ cup chopped onion

2 bell peppers, coarsely chopped (1 green and 1 yellow)

4 cloves garlic, minced

1 can (about 15 ounces) chickpeas, drained

1 can (about 14 ounces) stewed tomatoes, undrained

1 cup vegetable juice

¼ teaspoon red pepper flakes

½ cup (2 ounces) crumbled feta cheese

¼ cup chopped fresh basil

1. Heat oil in large saucepan over medium heat. Add onion; cook 5 minutes, stirring occasionally. Add bell peppers and garlic; cook 5 minutes, stirring occasionally.

2. Stir in chickpeas, tomatoes with juices, vegetable juice and red pepper flakes; bring to a boil over high heat. Reduce heat to low; simmer, uncovered, 12 minutes or until vegetables are tender.

3. Ladle into shallow bowls; top with feta cheese and basil.

Moroccan Lamb Stew

Makes 8 servings

- 2 pounds lamb for stew, cut into 1-inch pieces
- ½ teaspoon ground cinnamon
- ¼ teaspoon ground cloves
- ¼ teaspoon ground black pepper
- 1 tablespoon olive oil
- 1 large onion, chopped (about 1 cup)
- 4 cups SWANSON® Chicken Stock
- 1 cup dried lentils
- 2 medium potatoes, cut into cubes (about 2 cups)
  Hot cooked couscous
  Chopped fresh cilantro leaves
  Chopped tomatoes

1. Season the lamb with the cinnamon, cloves and black pepper.

2. Heat the oil in an 8-quart saucepot over medium-high heat. Add the lamb in 2 batches and cook until it's well browned, stirring often. Remove the lamb from the saucepot.

3. Reduce the heat to medium. Add the onion to the saucepot and cook until it's tender-crisp. Return the lamb to the saucepot. Stir in the stock and heat to a boil. Reduce the heat to low. Cover and cook for 1 hour.

4. Stir in the lentils and potatoes. Cook for 20 minutes or until the lamb is cooked through and the lentils and potatoes are tender. Serve over the couscous and sprinkle with the cilantro, if desired. Top with tomatoes.

Meat-Packed Favorites

Beef Vegetable Soup

Makes 6 to 8 servings

1½ pounds cubed beef stew meat

¼ cup all-purpose flour

3 tablespoons vegetable oil, divided

1 onion, chopped

2 stalks celery, chopped

3 tablespoons tomato paste

2 teaspoons salt

1 teaspoon dried thyme

½ teaspoon garlic powder

¼ teaspoon black pepper

6 cups beef broth, divided

1 can (28 ounces) stewed tomatoes, undrained

1 tablespoon Worcestershire sauce

1 bay leaf

4 unpeeled red potatoes (about 1 pound), cut into 1-inch pieces

3 medium carrots, cut in half lengthwise and cut into ½-inch slices

6 ounces green beans, trimmed and cut into 1-inch pieces

1 cup frozen corn

1. Combine beef and flour in medium bowl; toss to coat. Heat 1 tablespoon oil in large saucepan or Dutch oven over medium-high heat. Cook beef in two batches 5 minutes or until browned on all sides, adding additional 1 tablespoon oil after first batch. Remove beef to medium bowl.

2. Heat remaining 1 tablespoon oil in same saucepan. Add onion and celery; cook and stir 5 minutes or until softened. Add tomato paste, salt, thyme, garlic powder and pepper; cook and stir 1 minute. Stir in 1 cup broth, scraping up browned bits from bottom of saucepan. Stir in remaining 5 cups broth, tomatoes with juice, Worcestershire sauce, bay leaf and beef; bring to a boil.

3. Reduce heat to low; cover and simmer 1 hour and 20 minutes. Add potatoes and carrots; cook 15 minutes. Add green beans and corn; cook 15 minutes or until vegetables are tender. Remove and discard bay leaf before serving.

Chunky Chicken Stew ▶

Makes 2 servings

1 teaspoon olive oil

1 small onion, chopped

1 cup thinly sliced carrots

1 cup chicken broth

1 can (about 14 ounces) diced tomatoes

1 cup diced cooked chicken breast

3 cups sliced kale or baby spinach

1. Heat oil in large saucepan over medium-high heat. Add onion; cook and stir about 5 minutes or until golden brown. Stir in carrots and broth; bring to a boil. Reduce heat; simmer, uncovered, 5 minutes.

2. Stir in tomatoes; simmer 5 minutes or until carrots are tender. Add chicken; cook and stir until heated through. Add kale; stir until wilted.

Chicken and Sweet Potato Chili

Makes 4 servings

(pictured on page 96)

1 to 2 sweet potatoes, peeled and cut into ½-inch pieces

2 teaspoons canola oil

1 cup chopped onion

¾ pound boneless skinless chicken breasts or chicken tenders, cut into ¾-inch pieces*

3 cloves garlic, minced

2 teaspoons chili powder

1 can (about 14 ounces) diced fire-roasted tomatoes, undrained

1 can (about 15 ounces) kidney beans or pinto beans, drained

½ cup chipotle or jalapeño salsa

*This is easier to do if chicken is partially frozen.

1. Place sweet potatoes in large saucepan and add enough water to cover. Bring to a boil. Reduce heat to medium-low; simmer 5 minutes or until almost tender. Drain sweet potatoes; set aside. Heat oil in large saucepan over medium heat. Add onion; cook and stir 5 minutes.

2. Add chicken, garlic and chili powder; cook 3 minutes, stirring frequently. Add tomatoes with juice, beans, salsa and sweet potatoes; bring to a boil over high heat. Reduce heat to medium-low; simmer, uncovered, 10 minutes or until chicken is cooked through.

Meat-Packed Favorites

Smokey Chili with Corn-Cilantro Quinoa

Makes 8 servings

Chili

1 tablespoon canola oil

1 pound ground beef or turkey

2 cups coarsely chopped green bell peppers

1 cup chopped onion

2 cans (about 14 ounces each) stewed tomatoes

2 cans (about 15 ounces each) dark kidney beans, rinsed and drained

2½ cups water

2 teaspoons smoked paprika

3 teaspoons ground cumin, divided

Quinoa

1 cup uncooked quinoa, preferably tri-colored

1½ cups frozen corn

½ cup chopped fresh cilantro

Salt and black pepper

1 cup sour cream

1. For chili, heat oil in large saucepan or Dutch oven over medium-high heat. Add beef; cook 3 minutes or until just beginning to brown, stirring frequently. Stir in bell peppers and onion; cook 6 minutes or just until tender, stirring occasionally.

2. Stir in tomatoes, beans, water, paprika and 1 teaspoon cumin; bring to a boil. Reduce heat to medium-low, cook, uncovered, 30 minutes or until thickened. Remove from heat, stir in remaining 2 teaspoons cumin.

3. Meanwhile, cook quinoa with corn according to quinoa package directions. Remove from heat; stir in cilantro. Season with salt and black pepper.

4. Spoon quinoa mixture in bowls; top with chili and sour cream.

Tip

Don't underestimate the sour cream—it ties the flavors and ingredients together!

Chicken and Mushroom Stew

Makes 6 servings

4 tablespoons vegetable oil, divided

2 medium leeks (white and light green parts only), halved lengthwise and thinly sliced crosswise

1 carrot, cut into 1-inch pieces

1 stalk celery, diced

6 boneless, skinless chicken thighs (about 2 pounds)

Salt and black pepper

12 ounces cremini mushrooms, quartered

1 ounce dried porcini mushrooms, rehydrated in 1½ cups hot water and chopped, soaking liquid strained and reserved

¼ cup all-purpose flour

1 teaspoon minced garlic

1 sprig fresh thyme

1 bay leaf

½ cup dry white wine

1 cup chicken broth

Slow Cooker Directions

1. Heat 1 tablespoon oil in large skillet over medium heat. Add leeks; cook 8 minutes or until softened. Remove to slow cooker. Add carrot and celery.

2. Heat 1 tablespoon oil in same skillet over medium-high heat. Season chicken with salt and pepper. Add chicken in batches; cook 8 minutes or until browned on both sides. Remove to slow cooker.

3. Heat remaining 2 tablespoons oil in same skillet. Add cremini mushrooms; cook 7 minutes or until mushrooms have released their liquid and started to brown. Add porcini mushrooms, flour, garlic, thyme and bay leaf; cook and stir 1 minute. Add wine; cook and stir until evaporated, scraping up browned bits from bottom of skillet. Add reserved soaking liquid and broth; bring to a simmer. Pour mixture into slow cooker.

4. Cover; cook on HIGH 2 to 3 hours. Remove and discard thyme sprig and bay leaf before serving.

Sausage Rice Soup

Makes 4 to 6 servings

- 2 teaspoons olive oil
- 8 ounces Italian sausage, casings removed
- 1 small onion, chopped
- ½ teaspoon fennel seeds
- 1 tablespoon tomato paste
- 4 cups chicken broth
- 1 can (about 14 ounces) whole tomatoes, undrained, tomatoes crushed with hands or chopped
- 1½ cups water
- ½ cup uncooked rice
- ¼ teaspoon salt
- ⅛ teaspoon black pepper
- 2 to 3 ounces baby spinach
- ⅓ cup shredded mozzarella cheese (optional)

1. Heat oil in large saucepan or Dutch oven over medium-high heat. Add sausage; cook 8 minutes or until browned, stirring to break up meat. Add onion; cook and stir 5 minutes or until softened. Add fennel seeds; cook and stir 30 seconds. Add tomato paste; cook and stir 1 minute.

2. Stir in broth, tomatoes with juice, water, rice, ¼ teaspoon salt and ⅛ teaspoon pepper; bring to a boil. Reduce heat to medium-low. Cook 18 minutes or until rice is tender. Stir in spinach; cook 3 minutes or until wilted. Season with additional salt and pepper.

3. Sprinkle with cheese, if desired, just before serving.

Turkey Chili

Makes about 8 servings

2 tablespoons olive oil, divided

2 pounds ground turkey

2 onions, chopped

2 stalks celery, chopped

2 medium carrots, chopped

2 cloves garlic, minced

2 tablespoons chili powder

2 teaspoons ground cumin

1½ teaspoons salt

1 teaspoon Italian seasoning

1 teaspoon red pepper flakes

½ teaspoon black pepper

2 tablespoons tomato paste

1 can (28 ounces) tomato purée

1 container (32 ounces) chicken or vegetable broth

1 can (about 15 ounces) chickpeas

1 can (about 15 ounces) kidney beans

¾ cup corn (thawed if frozen)

¾ cup edamame (thawed if frozen)

1. Heat 1 tablespoon oil in large saucepan or Dutch oven over medium-high heat. Add turkey; cook 8 minutes or until no longer pink, stirring to break up meat. Remove to medium bowl; drain off any excess liquid.

2. Add remaining 1 tablespoon oil, onions, celery and carrots to saucepan; cook 10 minutes or until vegetables are softened, stirring frequently. Add garlic; cook and stir 1 minute. Add chili powder, cumin, salt, Italian seasoning, red pepper flakes and black pepper; cook and stir 1 minute. Stir in tomato paste; cook and stir 1 minute.

3. Return turkey to saucepan with tomato purée; mix well. Stir in broth and bring to a boil. Reduce heat to low; cook, uncovered, 30 minutes.

4. Add chickpeas, beans, corn and edamame; cook 20 minutes, stirring occasionally.

Beefy Broccoli & Cheese Soup ▶

Makes 4 servings

¼ pound ground beef

2 cups beef broth

1 bag (10 ounces) frozen chopped broccoli, thawed

¼ cup chopped onion

1 cup milk

2 tablespoons all-purpose flour

1 cup (4 ounces) shredded sharp Cheddar cheese

1½ teaspoons chopped fresh oregano *or* ½ teaspoon dried oregano

Salt and black pepper

Hot pepper sauce

1. Brown beef in large skillet over medium-high heat 6 to 8 minutes, stirring to break up meat. Drain fat.

2. Pour broth into medium saucepan; bring to a boil over medium-high heat. Add broccoli and onion; cook 5 minutes or until broccoli is tender. Stir milk into flour in small bowl until smooth. Stir milk mixture and ground beef into saucepan; cook and stir until mixture is thickened and heated through.

3. Add cheese and oregano; stir until cheese is melted. Season with salt, black pepper and hot pepper sauce.

Basil Pork and Green Bean Stew

Makes 6 servings

1 package (9 ounces) frozen cut green beans

3½ cups peeled red potatoes, cut into ½-inch cubes

1 pound trimmed pork tenderloin, cut into 1-inch cubes

1 cup prepared meatless spaghetti sauce

½ teaspoon salt

1 tablespoon chopped fresh basil *or* 1 teaspoon dried basil

¼ cup grated Parmesan cheese

Microwave Directions

1. Place beans in 10- to 12-inch or 4-quart glass microwavable casserole. Microwave, covered, at HIGH 2 minutes. Drain in colander.

2. Using same dish, microwave potatoes, covered, on HIGH 4 minutes. Stir in pork, beans, spaghetti sauce and salt. Microwave on HIGH 10 minutes, stirring halfway through. Stir in basil. Microwave 5 to 7 minutes or until potatoes are tender and meat is no longer pink in center. Serve with cheese.

Skillet Chicken Soup

Makes 6 servings

1 teaspoon paprika

½ teaspoon salt

¼ teaspoon black pepper

¾ pound boneless skinless chicken breasts or thighs, cut into ¾-inch pieces

2 teaspoons vegetable oil

1 large onion, chopped

1 red bell pepper, cut into ½-inch pieces

3 cloves garlic, minced

3 cups reduced-sodium chicken broth

1 can (19 ounces) cannellini beans or small white beans, rinsed and drained

3 cups sliced savoy or napa cabbage

½ cup herb-flavored croutons, slightly crushed (optional)

1. Combine paprika, salt and black pepper in medium bowl; stir to blend. Add chicken; toss to coat.

2. Heat oil in large deep nonstick skillet over medium-high heat. Add chicken, onion, bell pepper and garlic; cook and stir 8 minutes or until chicken is cooked through.

3. Add broth and beans; bring to a simmer. Cover and simmer 5 minutes. Stir in cabbage; cover and simmer 3 minutes or until cabbage is wilted. Ladle evenly into six shallow bowls. Top evenly with crushed croutons, if desired.

Tip

Savoy cabbage, also called curly cabbage, is round with pale green crinkled leaves. Napa cabbage is also known as Chinese cabbage and is elongated with light green stalks.

Beer-Braised Chili

Makes about 8 to 10 servings

- 2 tablespoons canola or vegetable oil
- 2 pounds boneless beef chuck roast or stew meat, cut into ¾-inch cubes
- 1 large onion, chopped
- 4 cloves garlic, minced
- 1 tablespoon chili powder
- 1 tablespoon ground cumin
- 1¼ teaspoons salt
- 1 teaspoon dried oregano
- ½ teaspoon ground red pepper
- 1 can (about 14 ounces) Mexican-style stewed tomatoes, undrained
- 1 bottle or can (12 ounces) beer (not dark beer)
- ½ cup salsa
- 1 can (about 15 ounces) black beans, rinsed and drained
- 1 can (about 15 ounces) red beans or pinto beans, rinsed and drained

Optional toppings: chopped fresh cilantro, thinly sliced green onions, shredded Chihuahua or Cheddar cheese, sliced pickled jalapeño peppers and/or sour cream

1. Heat oil in large saucepan or Dutch oven over medium-high heat. Add beef, onion and garlic; cook 5 minutes, stirring occasionally. Sprinkle with chili powder, cumin, salt, oregano and ground red pepper; mix well. Add tomatoes with juice, beer and salsa; bring to a boil. Reduce heat to low; cover and simmer 1¼ hours or until beef is very tender, stirring once.

2. Stir in beans. Simmer, uncovered, 20 minutes or until thickened as desired. Top as desired.

Acorn Squash Soup with Chicken and Red Pepper Meatballs

Makes 2 servings

1 small to medium acorn squash (about ¾ pound)

½ pound ground chicken or turkey

1 red bell pepper, seeded and finely chopped

1 egg, lightly beaten

1 teaspoon dried parsley flakes

1 teaspoon ground coriander

½ teaspoon black pepper

¼ teaspoon ground cinnamon

3 cups reduced-sodium vegetable broth

2 tablespoons sour cream (optional)

Ground red pepper (optional)

1. Pierce squash skin with fork. Place in microwavable dish; microwave on HIGH 8 to 10 minutes or until tender. Cool 10 minutes.

2. Meanwhile, combine chicken, bell pepper, egg, parsley flakes, coriander, black pepper and cinnamon in large bowl; mix lightly. Shape mixture into eight meatballs. Place meatballs in microwavable dish; microwave on HIGH 5 minutes or until cooked through. Set aside to cool.

3. Remove and discard seeds from cooled squash. Scrape squash flesh from shell into large saucepan; mash squash with potato masher. Add broth and meatballs to saucepan; cook over medium-high heat 12 minutes, stirring occasionally. Add additional liquid if necessary.

4. Garnish each serving with 1 tablespoon sour cream and ground red pepper.

Red Bean Soup with Andouille Sausage

Makes 6 to 8 servings

2 tablespoons butter

1 large onion, diced

3 stalks celery, diced

2 cloves garlic, chopped

8 cups chicken broth

1½ cups dried red kidney beans, soaked in cold water 1 hour, rinsed and drained

1 ham hock

1 bay leaf

2 parsnips, diced

1 sweet potato, peeled and diced

1 pound andouille sausage or kielbasa, sliced ½ inch thick

Salt and black pepper

Slow Cooker Directions

1. Melt butter in large saucepan over medium heat. Add onion, celery and garlic; cook and stir 5 minutes or until tender; remove to slow cooker. Add broth, beans, ham hock and bay leaf. Cover; cook on HIGH 2 hours.

2. Remove ham hock; let stand until cool enough to handle. Remove ham from hock; chop and return to slow cooker. Discard bone. Add parsnips and sweet potato. Cover; cook on HIGH 2 hours.

3. Add sausage. Cover; cook on HIGH 30 minutes or until heated through. Remove and discard bay leaf. Season with salt and pepper.

Roasted Corn and Chicken Soup

Makes 8 servings

4 tablespoons olive oil, divided

1 can (15 ounces) yellow corn, drained

1 can (15 ounces) white corn, drained

1 onion, diced

3 tablespoons ORTEGA® Fire-Roasted Diced Green Chiles

½ of 1½- to 2-pound cooked rotisserie chicken, bones removed and meat shredded

1 packet (1.25 ounces) ORTEGA® 40% Less Sodium Taco Seasoning Mix

4 cups chicken broth

4 ORTEGA® Yellow Corn Taco Shells, crumbled

HEAT 2 tablespoons oil over medium heat in large skillet until hot. Add corn. Cook 8 minutes or until browned; stir often to prevent corn from burning. Add remaining 2 tablespoons oil, onion and chiles. Cook and stir 3 minutes longer.

TRANSFER mixture to large pot. Stir in shredded chicken. Add seasoning mix and toss to combine. Stir in chicken broth and bring to a boil. Reduce heat to low. Simmer 15 minutes. Serve with crumbled taco shells.

Tip

To make sure the canned corn is well drained, press excess water out with a paper towel.

Spicy Pork Stew with Roasted Veggies

Makes 8 servings

1	teaspoon olive oil
1½	pounds boneless pork loin, trimmed and cut into ½-inch cubes
1	cup chopped onion
2	red bell peppers, cut into ½-inch pieces
1	container (8 ounces) sliced mushrooms
1	medium acorn squash, peeled and cut into ½-inch cubes
1	can (about 14 ounces) diced tomatoes
1	can (about 14 ounces) chicken broth
½	teaspoon red pepper flakes
½	teaspoon black pepper
½	teaspoon dried thyme
	Fresh oregano (optional)

1. Heat oil in Dutch oven over medium-high heat. Add half of pork; cook 5 minutes or until browned, stirring occasionally. Repeat with remaining pork.

2. Add onion, bell peppers and mushrooms to Dutch oven. Stir in squash, tomatoes, broth, red pepper flakes, black pepper and thyme; bring to a boil over high heat. Reduce heat to medium-low; cover and simmer 1 hour or until pork is tender. Garnish with oregano.

Black Bean, Corn and Turkey Chili

Makes 6 servings

1 tablespoon vegetable oil

1 pound ground turkey

1 large onion, chopped (about 1 cup)

2 tablespoons chili powder

1 teaspoon ground cumin

1 teaspoon dried oregano leaves, crushed

½ teaspoon ground black pepper

¼ teaspoon garlic powder or 2 cloves garlic, minced

1¾ cups SWANSON® Chicken Stock

1 cup PACE® Picante Sauce

1 tablespoon sugar

1 can (about 15 ounces) black beans, rinsed and drained

1 can (about 16 ounces) whole kernel corn, drained

1. Heat the oil in a 4-quart saucepan over medium-high heat. Add the turkey, onion, chili powder, cumin, oregano, black pepper and garlic powder. Cook until the turkey is well browned, stirring often to separate the meat.

2. Stir the stock, picante sauce, sugar, beans and corn in the saucepan and heat to a boil. Reduce the heat to low. Cover and cook for 30 minutes or until the mixture is hot and bubbling.

Serving Suggestion

Serve with warm restaurant-style tortilla chips. For dessert, serve with sliced watermelon and brownies.

Confetti Chicken Chili ▶

Makes 5 servings

1 pound ground chicken or turkey

1 large onion, chopped

3½ cups chicken broth

1 can (about 15 ounces) Great Northern beans, rinsed and drained

2 carrots, chopped

1 medium green bell pepper, chopped

2 plum tomatoes, chopped

1 jalapeño pepper, finely chopped (optional)

2 teaspoons chili powder

½ teaspoon ground red pepper

1. Spray large saucepan with nonstick cooking spray; heat over medium heat. Add chicken and onion; cook and stir 5 minutes or until chicken is browned. Drain fat.

2. Add broth, beans, carrots, bell pepper, tomatoes, jalapeño pepper, chili powder and ground red pepper to saucepan; bring to a boil. Reduce heat to low; cover and simmer 15 minutes.

Pork and Red Bean Chili

Makes 4 servings

1 tablespoon canola or vegetable oil

1 pound pork tenderloin, cut into ½-inch pieces

4 cloves garlic, minced

2 teaspoons chili powder

1 can (about 14 ounces) fire-roasted diced tomatoes

¾ cup jalapeño salsa

1 can (about 15 ounces) red kidney beans, rinsed and drained

½ cup chopped fresh cilantro

1. Heat oil in large saucepan over medium heat. Add pork, garlic and chili powder; cook 4 minutes or until pork is browned on all sides, stirring occasionally.

2. Add tomatoes and salsa; bring to a boil over medium heat. Reduce heat to low; simmer, uncovered, 10 minutes or until pork is no longer pink in center.

3. Stir in beans; simmer 3 minutes or until heated through. Ladle into bowls; top with cilantro.

Spoonfuls of Noodles

Pasta e Ceci

Makes 4 servings

- 4 tablespoons olive oil, divided
- 1 onion, chopped
- 1 carrot, chopped
- 1 clove garlic, minced
- 1 sprig fresh rosemary
- 1 teaspoon salt, plus additional for seasoning
- 1 can (28 ounces) whole tomatoes, drained and crushed (see Note)
- 2 cups vegetable broth
- 1 can (about 15 ounces) chickpeas, undrained
- 1 bay leaf
- ⅛ teaspoon red pepper flakes
- 1 cup uncooked orecchiette pasta
  Black pepper (optional)
  Chopped fresh parsley or basil (optional)

1. Heat 3 tablespoons oil in large saucepan over medium-high heat. Add onion and carrot; cook 10 minutes or until vegetables are softened, stirring occasionally.

2. Add garlic, rosemary and 1 teaspoon salt; cook and stir 1 minute. Stir in tomatoes, broth, chickpeas with liquid, bay leaf and red pepper flakes. Remove 1 cup mixture to food processor or blender; process until smooth. Stir back into saucepan; bring to a boil.

3. Stir in pasta. Reduce heat to medium; cook 12 to 15 minutes or until pasta is tender and mixture is creamy. Remove and discard bay leaf and rosemary sprig. Taste and season with additional salt and black pepper, if desired. Divide evenly among bowls; garnish with parsley and drizzle with remaining 1 tablespoon oil.

Note

To crush the tomatoes, take them out of the can one at a time and crush them between your fingers over the pot. Or coarsely chop them with a knife.

Chicken and Gnocchi Soup

Makes 6 to 8 servings

¼ cup (½ stick) butter

1 tablespoon extra virgin olive oil

1 cup finely diced onion

2 stalks celery, finely chopped

2 cloves garlic, minced

¼ cup all-purpose flour

4 cups half-and-half

1 can (about 14 ounces) chicken broth

1 teaspoon salt

½ teaspoon dried thyme

½ teaspoon dried parsley flakes

¼ teaspoon ground nutmeg

1 package (about 16 ounces) uncooked gnocchi

1 package (6 ounces) fully cooked chicken strips, chopped *or* 1 cup diced cooked chicken

1 cup shredded carrots

1 cup coarsely chopped fresh spinach

1. Melt butter in large saucepan or Dutch oven over medium heat; add oil. Add onion, celery and garlic; cook 8 minutes or until vegetables are softened and onion is translucent, stirring occasionally.

2. Whisk in flour; cook and stir 1 minute. Whisk in half-and-half; cook 15 minutes or until thickened, stirring occasionally.

3. Whisk in broth, salt, thyme, parsley flakes and nutmeg; cook 10 minutes or until soup is slightly thickened, stirring occasionally. Add gnocchi, chicken, carrots and spinach; cook 5 minutes or until gnocchi are heated through.

Sausage Vegetable Rotini Soup ▶

Makes 4 servings

1 tablespoon olive oil

6 ounces bulk pork sausage

1 cup chopped onion

1 cup chopped green bell pepper

3 cups water

1 can (about 14 ounces) diced tomatoes

¼ cup ketchup

2 teaspoons beef bouillon granules

2 teaspoons chili powder

4 ounces uncooked tri-colored rotini pasta

1 cup frozen corn, thawed and drained

1. Heat oil in large saucepan over medium-high heat. Add sausage; cook 3 minutes or until no longer pink, stirring to break up sausage. Drain fat. Add onion and bell pepper; cook and stir 3 to 4 minutes or until onion is translucent.

2. Add water, tomatoes, ketchup, beef bouillon and chili powder; bring to a boil over high heat. Stir in pasta; return to a boil. Reduce heat to medium-low; simmer, uncovered, 12 minutes. Stir in corn; cook 2 minutes or until pasta is tender and corn is heated through.

One-Pot Chinese Chicken Soup

Makes 4 servings

(pictured on page 128)

6 cups chicken broth

2 cups water

1 pound boneless skinless chicken thighs

⅓ cup reduced-sodium soy sauce

1 package (16 ounces) frozen stir-fry vegetables

6 ounces uncooked dried thin Chinese egg noodles

1 to 3 tablespoons sriracha sauce

1. Combine broth, water, chicken and soy sauce in medium saucepan; bring to a boil over high heat. Reduce heat to low; cover and simmer 20 minutes or until chicken is cooked through and very tender. Remove to bowl; let stand until cool enough to handle.

2. Meanwhile, add vegetables and noodles to broth in saucepan; bring to a boil over high heat. Reduce heat to medium-high; cook 5 minutes or until noodles are tender and vegetables are heated through, stirring frequently.

3. Shred chicken into bite-size pieces. Stir chicken and 1 tablespoon sriracha into soup; taste and add additional sriracha for a spicier flavor.

Pasta Fagioli Soup

Makes 5 to 6 servings

2 cans (about 14 ounces each) reduced-sodium vegetable broth

1 can (about 15 ounces) Great Northern beans, rinsed and drained

1 can (about 14 ounces) diced tomatoes

2 zucchini, quartered lengthwise and sliced

1 tablespoon olive oil

1½ teaspoons minced garlic

½ teaspoon dried basil

½ teaspoon dried oregano

½ cup uncooked tubetti, ditalini or small shell pasta

½ cup garlic seasoned croutons

½ cup grated Asiago or Romano cheese

3 tablespoons chopped fresh basil or Italian parsley (optional)

Slow Cooker Directions

1. Combine broth, beans, tomatoes, zucchini, oil, garlic, dried basil and oregano in slow cooker; mix well. Cover; cook on LOW 3 to 4 hours.

2. Stir in pasta. Cover; cook on LOW 1 hour or until pasta is tender.

3. Serve soup with croutons and cheese. Garnish with fresh basil.

Tip

Only small pasta varieties like tubetti, ditalini or small shell-shaped pasta should be used in this recipe. The low heat of a slow cooker won't allow larger pasta shapes to cook completely.

Ramen Chili

Makes 8 to 10 servings

2 teaspoons vegetable oil

2 pounds ground beef

2 red onions, diced

1 red bell pepper, diced

6 tablespoons chili powder

4 teaspoons salt

2 teaspoons ground cumin

¼ teaspoon ground red pepper

4 cans (about 14 ounces each) diced tomatoes with basil, garlic and oregano

2 cans (about 15 ounces each) kidney beans, rinsed and drained

2 cups water

1 package (3 ounces) ramen noodles, any flavor, broken*

1 tablespoon packed light brown sugar

Optional toppings: sour cream, shredded Cheddar cheese and thinly sliced green onions

Discard seasoning packet.

1. Heat oil in Dutch oven over medium-high heat. Add beef; brown 6 to 8 minutes, stirring to break up meat. Remove to large bowl with slotted spoon. Add onions and bell pepper to Dutch oven; cook 6 minutes or until softened. Add chili powder, salt, cumin and ground red pepper; cook and stir 1 minute.

2. Return beef to Dutch oven; stir in tomatoes, beans, water, noodles and brown sugar. Bring to a boil; reduce heat to medium-low and simmer 45 minutes to 1 hour, stirring occasionally. Top as desired.

Greek-Style Chicken Stew

Makes 6 servings

2 cups sliced mushrooms

2 cups cubed peeled eggplant

1¼ cups reduced-sodium chicken broth

¾ cup coarsely chopped onion

2 cloves garlic, minced

1½ teaspoons all-purpose flour, plus additional for dusting

1 teaspoon dried oregano

½ teaspoon dried basil

½ teaspoon dried thyme

6 skinless chicken breast, (about 2 pounds)

3 tablespoons dry sherry or reduced-sodium chicken broth

¼ teaspoon salt

¼ teaspoon black pepper

1 can (14 ounces) artichoke hearts, drained

12 ounces uncooked wide egg noodles

Slow Cooker Directions

1. Combine mushrooms, eggplant, broth, onion, garlic, 1½ teaspoons flour, oregano, basil and thyme in slow cooker. Cover; cook on HIGH 1 hour.

2. Coat chicken very lightly with additional flour. Generously spray large skillet with nonstick cooking spray; heat over medium heat. Cook chicken 10 to 15 minutes or until browned on all sides.

3. Remove vegetables to bowl using slotted spoon. Layer chicken in slow cooker; return vegetables to slow cooker. Add sherry, salt and pepper. Turn slow cooker to LOW. Cover; cook on LOW 6 to 6½ hours or until chicken is no longer pink in center and vegetables are tender.

4. Stir in artichokes; cover and cook on LOW 45 minutes to 1 hour or until heated through. Cook noodles according to package directions. Serve chicken stew over noodles.

Mexican Turkey Chili Mac ▶

Makes 6 servings

1 pound ground turkey

1 package (1¼ ounces) reduced-sodium taco seasoning mix

1 can (14½ ounces) reduced-sodium stewed tomatoes

1 can (11 ounces) corn with red and green peppers, undrained

1½ cups cooked elbow macaroni, without salt, drained

1 ounce low-salt corn chips, crushed

½ cup shredded reduced-fat Cheddar cheese

1. In large nonstick skillet, over medium-high heat, sauté turkey 5 to 6 minutes or until no longer pink; drain. Stir in taco seasoning, tomatoes, corn and macaroni. Reduce heat to medium and cook 4 to 5 minutes until heated through.

2. Sprinkle corn chips over meat mixture and top with cheese. Cover and heat 1 to 2 minutes or until cheese is melted.

National Turkey Federation

Pork and Noodle Soup

Makes 6 servings

1 package (1 ounce) dried shiitake mushrooms

4 ounces uncooked thin egg noodles

6 cups chicken broth

2 cloves garlic, minced

½ cup shredded carrots

4 ounces ham or Canadian bacon, cut into short, thin strips

1 tablespoon hoisin sauce

⅛ teaspoon black pepper

2 tablespoons minced fresh chives

1. Place mushrooms in small bowl; cover with warm water. Soak 20 minutes to soften. Drain mushrooms; squeeze out excess water. Discard stems; slice caps.

2. Meanwhile, cook egg noodles according to package directions until tender; drain.

3. Combine broth and garlic in large saucepan; bring to a boil over high heat. Reduce heat to low. Stir in mushrooms, carrots, ham, hoisin sauce and pepper; simmer 15 minutes. Stir in noodles; cook until heated through. Sprinkle with chives just before serving.

Roasted Chicken with Caramelized Onions Soup

Makes 6 servings

2 teaspoons vegetable oil

2 medium onions, halved and thinly sliced (about 1 cup)

8 cups SWANSON® Chicken Broth (Regular, Natural Goodness® or Certified Organic)

⅛ teaspoon ground black pepper

2 medium carrots, sliced (about 1 cup)

2 stalks celery, sliced (about 1 cup)

¾ cup uncooked trumpet-shaped pasta (campanelle)

2 cups shredded roasted chicken

1. Heat the oil in a 10-inch skillet over medium-high heat. Add the onions and cook until they begin to brown, stirring occasionally. Reduce the heat to medium. Cook until the onions are tender and caramelized, stirring occasionally. Remove the skillet from the heat.

2. Heat the broth, pepper, carrots and celery in a 4-quart saucepan over medium-high heat to a boil. Stir the pasta and chicken into the saucepan. Reduce heat to medium and cook for 10 minutes or until the pasta is tender. Stir in the onions and serve immediately.

Kitchen Tip

Cut the peeled onions in half lengthwise. Place the halves cut-side down on the cutting surface. Slice **each** onion half with parallel cuts up to, but not through, the root. Cut the root end off to free the slices.

Hearty Meatball Stew

Makes 6 servings

- 1 pound ground turkey breast or extra-lean ground beef
- ¾ cup QUAKER® Oats (quick or old fashioned, uncooked)
- 1 can (8 ounces) no-salt-added tomato sauce, divided
- 1½ teaspoons garlic powder
- 1½ teaspoons dried thyme leaves, divided
- 2 cans (14½ ounces each) 70% less sodium, fat-free chicken broth
- ¾ teaspoon salt (optional)
- 2½ cups any frozen vegetable blend (do not thaw)
- ⅓ cup ditalini or other small pasta, uncooked
- ¼ cup water
- 2 tablespoons cornstarch

1. Heat broiler. Lightly spray rack of broiler pan with nonstick cooking spray.

2. Combine turkey, oats, ⅓ cup tomato sauce, garlic powder and 1 teaspoon thyme in large bowl; mix lightly but thoroughly. Transfer to sheet of aluminum foil or waxed paper. Pat mixture into 9×6-inch rectangle. Cut into 1½-inch squares; roll each square into a ball. Arrange meatballs on broiler pan.

3. Broil meatballs 6 to 8 inches from heat about 6 minutes or until cooked through, turning once.

4. While meatballs cook, bring broth, remaining tomato sauce, remaining ½ teaspoon thyme and salt, if desired, to a boil in 4-quart saucepan or Dutch oven over medium-high heat. Add vegetables and pasta; return to a boil. Reduce heat, cover and simmer 10 minutes or until vegetables and pasta are tender. Stir together water and cornstarch in small bowl until smooth. Add to pan along with meatballs. Cook and stir until broth is thickened. Spoon into bowls.

Chicken and Homemade Noodle Soup

Makes 4 servings

¾ cup all-purpose flour

2 teaspoons finely chopped fresh thyme *or* ½ teaspoon dried thyme, divided

¼ teaspoon salt

1 egg yolk, beaten

2 cups plus 3 tablespoons cold water, divided

1 pound boneless skinless chicken thighs, cut into ½- to ¾-inch pieces

5 cups chicken broth

1 onion, chopped

1 carrot, thinly sliced

¾ cup frozen peas

Chopped fresh Italian parsley

1. For noodles, combine flour, 1 teaspoon thyme and salt in small bowl. Stir in egg yolk and 3 tablespoons water until well blended. Shape into a small ball. Place dough on lightly floured surface; flatten slightly. Knead 5 minutes or until dough is smooth and elastic, adding more flour to prevent sticking, if necessary. Cover with plastic wrap. Let stand 15 minutes.

2. Roll out dough to ⅛-inch thickness or thinner on lightly floured surface. If dough is too elastic, let rest several minutes. Let dough rest about 30 minutes to dry slightly. Cut into ¼-inch-wide strips. Cut strips 1½ to 2 inches long; set aside.

3. Combine chicken and remaining 2 cups water in medium saucepan. Bring to a boil over high heat. Reduce heat to medium-low; cover and simmer 5 minutes or until chicken is cooked through. Drain chicken.

4. Combine broth, onion, carrot and remaining 1 teaspoon thyme in Dutch oven or large saucepan. Bring to a boil over high heat. Add noodles. Reduce heat to medium-low; simmer, uncovered, 8 minutes or until noodles are tender. Stir in chicken and peas; bring to a boil. Sprinkle with parsley.

Beef Stew

Makes 8 servings

3 pounds boneless beef chuck, trimmed and cut into 2-inch pieces

2 teaspoons salt

½ teaspoon black pepper

2 tablespoons olive or vegetable oil

3 medium sweet or yellow onions, halved and sliced

6 medium carrots, cut into ½-inch pieces

8 ounces sliced mushrooms

¼ pound smoked ham, cut into ¼-inch pieces

2 tablespoons minced garlic

1 can (about 15 ounces) stout

1 can (about 14 ounces) beef broth

1 teaspoon sugar

1 teaspoon herbes de Provence or dried thyme

1 teaspoon Worcestershire sauce

⅓ cup cold water

2 tablespoons cornstarch

3 tablespoons chopped fresh parsley

Hot cooked wide egg noodles

1. Season beef with salt and pepper. Heat oil in Dutch oven over medium-high heat. Add half of beef; cook 8 minutes or until browned on all sides. Remove to bowl; repeat with remaining half of beef.

2. Add onions; cook and stir 10 minutes over medium heat. Add carrots, mushrooms, ham and garlic; cook and stir 10 minutes or until vegetables are softened, scraping up browned bits from bottom of Dutch oven.

3. Return beef to Dutch oven and pour in stout and broth. (Liquid should just cover beef and vegetables; add water if needed.) Stir in sugar, herbes de Provence and Worcestershire sauce; bring to a boil. Reduce heat to low; cover and simmer 2 hours or until beef is fork-tender.

4. Skim fat. Stir water into cornstarch in small bowl until smooth. Whisk into stew; simmer 5 minutes. Stir in parsley. Serve over noodles.

Italian Hillside Garden Soup

Makes 6 servings

1 tablespoon olive oil

1 cup chopped onion

1 cup chopped green bell pepper

½ cup sliced celery

2 cans (about 14 ounces each) chicken broth

1 can (about 15 ounces) navy beans, rinsed and drained

1 can (about 14 ounces) diced tomatoes with basil, garlic and oregano

1 medium zucchini, chopped

1 cup frozen cut green beans, thawed

¼ teaspoon garlic powder

1 package (9 ounces) refrigerated sausage- or cheese-filled tortellini

3 tablespoons chopped fresh basil

Grated Asiago or Parmesan cheese (optional)

Slow Cooker Directions

1. Heat oil in large skillet over medium-high heat. Add onion, bell pepper and celery; cook and stir 4 minutes or until onion is translucent. Remove to slow cooker.

2. Add broth, navy beans, tomatoes, zucchini, green beans and garlic powder. Cover; cook on LOW 7 hours or on HIGH 3½ hours.

3. Add tortellini; cook on HIGH 20 minutes or until pasta is tender. Stir in basil. Sprinkle with cheese, if desired, just before serving.

Catalonian Stew

Makes 6 servings

- 2 boneless skinless chicken breasts, cut into bite-size pieces
- 3 ounces pepperoni, diced
- 1 tablespoon vegetable oil
- 2 cans (15 ounces each) tomato sauce
- 3 cups chicken broth
- 1 cup pimiento-stuffed green olives, halved
- 2 tablespoons sugar
- 8 ounces uncooked rotini or other shaped pasta
- ⅓ cup chopped fresh parsley
- ⅛ teaspoon crushed saffron (optional)
- 1 cup (4 ounces) SARGENTO® Traditional Cut Shredded Mild Cheddar Cheese or SARGENTO® Traditional Cut Shredded Sharp Cheddar Cheese
- 1 cup (4 ounces) SARGENTO® Fine Cut Shredded Monterey Jack Cheese

In Dutch oven, cook chicken and pepperoni in oil over medium heat until chicken is lightly browned, about 5 minutes; drain. Add tomato sauce, chicken broth, olives and sugar. Bring to a boil; reduce heat and simmer, covered, 15 minutes. Return to a boil. Add rotini, parsley and saffron, if desired; cover and cook an additional 15 minutes or until pasta is tender. Combine Cheddar and Monterey Jack cheeses in small bowl. Spoon stew into 6 individual ovenproof serving bowls; sprinkle evenly with cheese. Bake in preheated 350°F oven about 5 minutes or until cheese is melted.

All-in-One Burger Stew ▶

Makes 6 servings

1 pound ground beef

2 cups frozen Italian-style vegetables

1 can (about 14 ounces) diced tomatoes with basil and garlic

1 can (about 14 ounces) beef broth

2½ cups uncooked medium egg noodles

Salt and black pepper

Chopped fresh parsley (optional)

1. Brown beef in Dutch oven or large skillet over medium-high heat 6 to 8 minutes, stirring to break up meat. Drain fat.

2. Add vegetables, tomatoes and broth; bring to a boil over high heat.

3. Stir in noodles. Reduce heat to medium; cover and cook 12 to 15 minutes or until vegetables and noodles are tender. Season with salt and pepper. Garnish with parsley.

Serving Suggestions

To complete this meal, serve with breadsticks or a loaf of Italian bread and a simple salad.

Asian Noodle Soup

Makes 4 servings

4 ounces uncooked dried Chinese egg noodles

3 cans (about 14 ounces each) chicken broth

2 slices fresh ginger

2 cloves garlic, cut into halves

½ cup fresh snow peas, cut into 1-inch pieces

3 tablespoons chopped green onions

1 tablespoon chopped fresh cilantro

1½ teaspoons hot chili oil

½ teaspoon dark sesame oil

1. Cook noodles according to package directions, omitting salt. Drain and set aside.

2. Combine broth, ginger and garlic in large saucepan; bring to a boil over high heat. Reduce heat to low; simmer 15 minutes. Remove and discard ginger and garlic.

3. Add snow peas, green onions, cilantro, chili oil and sesame oil to broth; simmer 3 to 5 minutes. Stir in noodles; heat through.

Vegetarian Variety

Garden Vegetable Soup

Makes 8 to 10 servings

1 tablespoon olive oil

1 medium onion, chopped

1 carrot, chopped

1 stalk celery, chopped

1 medium zucchini, diced

1 medium yellow squash, diced

1 red bell pepper, diced

2 tablespoons tomato paste

2 cloves garlic, minced

2 teaspoons salt

1 teaspoon Italian seasoning

½ teaspoon black pepper

8 cups vegetable broth

1 can (28 ounces) whole tomatoes, chopped and juice reserved

½ cup uncooked pearl barley

1 cup cut green beans (1-inch pieces)

½ cup corn

¼ cup slivered fresh basil

1 tablespoon lemon juice

1. Heat oil in large saucepan or Dutch oven over medium-high heat. Add onion, carrot and celery; cook and stir 8 minutes or until vegetables are softened. Add zucchini, yellow squash and bell pepper; cook and stir 5 minutes or until softened. Stir in tomato paste, garlic, salt, Italian seasoning and black pepper; cook 1 minute. Stir in broth and tomatoes with juice; bring to a boil. Stir in barley.

2. Reduce heat to low; cook 30 minutes. Stir in green beans and corn; cook 15 minutes or until barley is tender and green beans are crisp-tender. Stir in basil and lemon juice.

Quick Broccoli Soup ▶

Makes 6 servings

4 cups reduced-sodium vegetable broth

2½ pounds broccoli florets

1 onion, quartered

1 cup milk

¼ teaspoon salt

¼ cup crumbled blue cheese

1. Place broth, broccoli and onion in large saucepan; bring to a boil over high heat. Reduce heat to low; cover and simmer 20 minutes or until vegetables are tender.

2. Blend soup with hand-held immersion blender until smooth. (Or process soup in batches in food processor or blender.) Stir in milk, salt and additional broth, if needed.

3. Ladle soup into serving bowls; sprinkle with cheese.

Roasted Tomato-Basil Soup

Makes 6 servings

(pictured on page 158)

2 cans (28 ounces each) whole tomatoes, drained and juice reserved (about 3 cups juice)

2½ tablespoons packed dark brown sugar

1 onion, finely chopped

3 cups chicken broth

3 tablespoons tomato paste

¼ teaspoon ground allspice

1 can (5 ounces) evaporated milk

¼ cup chopped fresh basil, plus additional for garnish

Salt and black pepper

Onion slices (optional)

Slow Cooker Directions

1. Preheat oven to 450°F. Line baking sheet with foil; spray with nonstick cooking spray. Arrange tomatoes on foil in single layer. Sprinkle with brown sugar; top with chopped onion. Bake 25 to 30 minutes or until tomatoes look dry and are lightly browned. Let tomatoes cool slightly; finely chop.

2. Place tomato mixture, 3 cups reserved juice from tomatoes, broth, tomato paste and allspice in slow cooker; mix well. Cover; cook on LOW 8 hours or on HIGH 4 hours.

3. Add evaporated milk and ¼ cup basil; season with salt and pepper. Cook on HIGH 30 minutes or until heated through. Garnish with additional basil and onion slices.

Rainbow Vegetable Stew

Makes 4 to 6 servings

- 1 tablespoon olive oil
- 1 red onion, chopped
- 2 stalks celery, chopped
- 3 cloves garlic, minced
- 2 teaspoons salt, divided
- 4 cups vegetable broth
- 1 butternut squash (about 2 pounds), peeled and cut into ½-inch pieces
- 1 red bell pepper, chopped
- 1 green bell pepper, chopped
- 1 teaspoon ground cumin
- ½ teaspoon dried oregano
- ¼ teaspoon chipotle chili powder
- 1½ cups water
- ¾ cup uncooked tricolor or white quinoa
- ½ cup corn
- 1 can (about 15 ounces) black beans, rinsed and drained
- ½ cup chopped fresh parsley
- 1 tablespoon lime juice

1. Heat oil in large saucepan over medium-high heat. Add onion and celery; cook and stir 5 minutes or until vegetables are softened. Add garlic and 1½ teaspoons salt; cook and stir 30 seconds. Stir in broth, squash, bell peppers, cumin, oregano and chipotle chili powder; bring to a boil. Reduce heat to medium; simmer 20 minutes or until squash is tender.

2. Meanwhile, bring 1½ cups water, quinoa and remaining ½ teaspoon salt to a boil in medium saucepan. Reduce heat to low; cover and simmer 15 minutes or until quinoa is tender and water is absorbed.

3. Stir corn and beans into stew; cook 5 minutes or until heated through. Stir in parsley and lime juice. Serve with quinoa.

Creamy Tomato Soup ▶

Makes 6 servings

3 tablespoons olive oil, divided

2 tablespoons butter

1 large onion, finely chopped

2 cloves garlic, minced

2 teaspoons sugar

1 teaspoon salt

½ teaspoon dried oregano

2 cans (28 ounces each) peeled Italian plum tomatoes, undrained

4 cups ½-inch focaccia cubes (half of 9-ounce loaf)

½ teaspoon freshly ground black pepper

½ cup whipping cream

1. Heat 2 tablespoons oil and butter in large saucepan over medium-high heat. Add onion; cook and stir 5 minutes or until softened. Add garlic, sugar, salt and oregano; cook and stir 30 seconds. Stir in tomatoes with juice; bring to a boil. Reduce heat to medium-low; simmer 45 minutes, stirring occasionally.

2. Meanwhile, prepare croutons. Preheat oven to 350°F. Combine focaccia cubes, remaining 1 tablespoon oil and pepper in large bowl; toss to coat. Spread on large rimmed baking sheet. Bake 10 minutes or until bread cubes are golden brown.

3. Blend soup with hand-held immersion blender until smooth. (Or process soup in batches in food processor or blender.) Stir in cream; cook until heated through. Serve soup topped with croutons.

Chilled Cantaloupe Soup

Makes 4 servings

½ medium to large cantaloupe, rind removed, seeded and cut into cubes

¼ cup plain nonfat Greek yogurt

¾ cup half-and-half

Salt and white pepper

Slivered cantaloupe (optional)

1. Place cubed cantaloupe in food processor or blender; process until smooth. Add yogurt; process until blended.

2. Pour cantaloupe mixture into medium bowl; stir in half-and-half. Season with salt and pepper to taste. Refrigerate until ready to serve. Garnish with slivered cantaloupe.

Summer Honeydew Soup

Substitute ½ medium honeydew melon for the cantaloupe.

Tip

This refreshing soup makes a great first course.

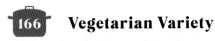

Curry Red Lentil and Chickpea Stew

Makes 6 servings

1 tablespoon olive oil

1 onion, chopped

3 cloves garlic, minced

2 tablespoons minced fresh ginger

1 tablespoon curry powder

2 teaspoons ground turmeric

1½ teaspoons salt

⅛ teaspoon ground red pepper

1 container (32 ounces) vegetable broth

1¼ cups uncooked red lentils (8 ounces)

1 can (about 15 ounces) chickpeas, rinsed and drained

1 can (14 ounces) coconut milk

1 package (5 ounces) baby spinach

1. Heat oil in large saucepan over medium-high heat. Add onion; cook and stir 5 minutes or until softened. Add garlic, ginger, curry powder, turmeric, salt and red pepper; cook and stir 1 minute. Add broth; bring to a boil. Stir in lentils; cook 15 minutes.

2. Stir in chickpeas and coconut milk; cook 5 to 10 minutes or until lentils are tender, chickpeas are heated through and stew is slightly thickened. Stir in spinach; cook and stir 3 minutes or just until spinach is wilted.

Coconut Cauliflower Cream Soup

Makes 6 servings

- 1 tablespoon coconut or vegetable oil
- 1 medium onion, chopped
- 1 tablespoon minced garlic
- 1 tablespoon minced fresh ginger
- 1 teaspoon salt
- 1 head cauliflower (1½ pounds), cut into florets
- 2 cans (about 13 ounces each) coconut milk, divided
- 1 cup water
- 1 teaspoon garam masala
- ½ teaspoon ground turmeric
- Optional toppings: hot chili oil, red pepper flakes and chopped fresh cilantro

1. Heat oil in large saucepan over medium-high heat. Add onion; cook and stir 5 minutes or until softened. Add garlic, ginger and salt; cook and stir 30 seconds.

2. Add cauliflower, 1 can coconut milk, water, garam masala and turmeric. Reduce heat to medium; cover and simmer 20 minutes or until cauliflower is very tender.

3. Remove from heat. Blend soup with immersion blender until smooth.* Return saucepan to medium heat; add 1 cup coconut milk. Cook and stir until heated through. Add additional coconut milk, if desired, to reach desired consistency. Top as desired.

Or blend soup in batches with blender or food processor, cooling to room temperature first if your appliance should not be used to blend hot liquids.

Vegetarian Quinoa Chili

Makes 4 to 6 servings

2 tablespoons vegetable oil

1 large onion

1 red bell pepper, diced

1 large carrot, peeled and diced

1 stalk celery, diced

1 jalapeño pepper, seeded and finely chopped

1 tablespoon minced garlic

1 tablespoon chili powder

2 teaspoons ground cumin

1 teaspoon kosher salt

1 can (about 15 ounces) kidney beans, rinsed and drained

1 can (28 ounces) crushed tomatoes

1 cup water

1 cup fresh or frozen corn

½ cup uncooked quinoa, rinsed well

Optional toppings: diced avocado, shredded Cheddar cheese and sliced green onions

1. Heat oil in large saucepan over medium-high heat. Add onion, bell pepper, carrot and celery; cook 10 minutes or until vegetables are softened, stirring occasionally. Add jalapeño pepper, garlic, chili powder, cumin and salt; cook 1 minute or until fragrant.

2. Add beans, tomatoes, water, corn and quinoa; bring to a boil. Reduce heat to low; cover and simmer 1 hour, stirring occasionally.

3. Spoon into bowls; top as desired.

Barley Stew with Cornmeal-Cheese Dumplings

Makes 4 servings

Stew

2 cans (11½ ounces each) spicy vegetable juice cocktail

1 can (about 15 ounces) butter beans, drained

1 can (about 14 ounces) stewed tomatoes, undrained

1 cup sliced zucchini

1 cup sliced carrots

1 cup water

½ cup chopped peeled parsnip

⅓ cup quick pearl barley

1 bay leaf

2 tablespoons chopped fresh thyme

1½ tablespoons chopped fresh rosemary leaves

Dumplings

⅓ cup all-purpose flour

⅓ cup cornmeal

1 teaspoon baking powder

¼ cup milk

1 tablespoon canola oil

⅓ cup shredded Cheddar cheese

1. For stew, combine vegetable juice, beans, tomatoes with juice, zucchini, carrots, water, parsnip, barley, bay leaf, thyme and rosemary in large saucepan. Bring to a boil over high heat. Reduce heat to medium-low. Cover; simmer 20 to 25 minutes or until tender, stirring occasionally. Remove and discard bay leaf.

2. For dumplings, combine flour, cornmeal and baking powder in small bowl. Combine milk and oil in separate small bowl; stir into flour mixture. Stir in cheese. Drop dough by spoonfuls to make four mounds onto boiling stew. Cover; simmer 10 to 12 minutes or until wooden toothpick inserted near center of dumpling comes out clean.

Vegetarian Variety

Zucchini Soup
with Herbed Cream

Makes 6 servings

½ cup sour cream

4 teaspoons chopped fresh basil leaves

4 teaspoons chopped fresh oregano leaves

2 tablespoons olive oil

1 large onion, finely chopped (about 1 cup)

1 clove garlic, minced

4 medium zucchini, thinly sliced (about 6 cups)

¼ teaspoon ground black pepper

3 cups SWANSON® Vegetable Broth (Regular **or** Certified Organic)

1. Stir the sour cream, **1 teaspoon** of the basil and **1 teaspoon** of the oregano in a small bowl. Cover and refrigerate.

2. Heat the oil in a 4-quart saucepan over medium heat. Add the onion and garlic and cook until they're tender. Add the zucchini and black pepper. Cook for 5 minutes or until the zucchini is tender.

3. Add the broth, remaining basil and remaining oregano. Heat to a boil. Reduce the heat to low. Cover and cook for 15 minutes.

4. Place ⅓ of the zucchini mixture into a blender or food processor. Cover and blend until smooth. Pour the mixture into a large bowl. Repeat the blending process twice more with the remaining zucchini mixture. Return all of the puréed mixture to the saucepan. Cook over medium heat for 5 minutes or until hot.

5. Divide the soup among 6 serving bowls and top with about 1 tablespoon of the sour cream mixture, using a spoon to swirl the cream in a decorative pattern on the soup surface.

Chickpea and Butternut Squash Stew

Makes 2 servings

1 teaspoon canola oil

¾ cup chopped onion

½ to 1 jalapeño pepper, seeded and minced

1 (½-inch) piece fresh ginger, peeled and minced

1 clove garlic, minced

2 teaspoons ground cumin

½ teaspoon ground coriander

1 cup cubed peeled butternut squash, sweet potato or pumpkin

1 cup canned chickpeas, rinsed and drained

½ cup water

1½ teaspoons soy sauce

1 cup coconut milk

Juice of 1 lime

¼ cup chopped fresh cilantro

Spinach leaves (optional)

1. Heat oil in medium saucepan over medium-low heat. Add onion, jalapeño pepper, ginger and garlic; cook and stir 2 to 3 minutes or until onion is translucent. Add cumin and coriander; cook and stir 1 minute.

2. Add squash, chickpeas, water and soy sauce to saucepan. Bring to a boil. Reduce heat and simmer 15 minutes or until squash is tender. Add coconut milk; cook and stir 2 to 3 minutes or until heated through. Stir in lime juice and cilantro. Garnish with spinach.

Fireball Vegetarian Chili

Makes 6 servings

- 1 tablespoon vegetable oil
- 1 onion, chopped
- 2 cloves garlic, minced
- 2 cans (15 to 19 ounces *each*) red kidney beans, rinsed and drained
- 1½ cups *each* coarsely chopped zucchini and carrots
- 1 can (15 ounces) crushed tomatoes in purée, undrained
- 1 can (7 ounces) whole kernel corn, drained
- 1 can (4½ ounces) chopped green chilies, drained
- ¼ cup FRANK'S® RedHot® Original Cayenne Pepper Sauce
- 1 tablespoon ground cumin

  Hot cooked rice

  Sour cream or shredded cheese

HEAT oil in large saucepot. Add onion and garlic and cook, stirring occasionally 3 minutes or just until tender. Stir in remaining ingredients except rice, sour cream and cheese.

HEAT to boiling. Reduce heat to medium-low. Cook, partially covered, 20 minutes or until vegetables are tender and flavors are blended. Serve with hot cooked rice. Garnish with sour cream or shredded cheese, if desired.

Tip

You can also serve chili over hot baked potatoes.

Groundnut Soup with Ginger and Cilantro

Makes 4 servings

1 tablespoon vegetable oil

1½ cups chopped onion

1 medium clove garlic, minced

2 teaspoons chili powder

1 teaspoon ground cumin

¼ teaspoon red pepper flakes

3 cups vegetable broth

1 can (about 14 ounces) diced tomatoes, undrained

8 ounces sweet potatoes, peeled and cut into ½-inch cubes

1 medium carrot, cut into ½-inch pieces

1 cup salted peanuts

1 tablespoon grated fresh ginger

¼ cup chopped fresh cilantro

1. Heat oil in large saucepan over medium-high heat. Add onion; cook and stir 4 minutes or until translucent. Add garlic, chili powder, cumin and red pepper flakes; cook and stir 15 seconds.

2. Add broth, tomatoes with juice, sweet potatoes and carrot; bring to a boil over high heat. Reduce heat to medium. Cover tightly; simmer 25 minutes or until vegetables are tender, stirring occasionally. Remove from heat. Stir in peanuts and ginger. Cool slightly.

3. Working in batches, process soup in blender or food processor until smooth. Return to saucepan. Heat over medium-high heat 2 minutes or until heated through. Sprinkle cilantro over each serving.

Creamy Roasted Poblano Soup

Makes 4 servings

6 large poblano peppers

1 tablespoon olive oil

¾ cup chopped onion

½ cup thinly sliced celery

½ cup thinly sliced carrots

1 clove garlic, minced

2 cans (about 14 ounces each) vegetable broth

1 package (8 ounces) cream cheese, cubed

Salt and black pepper

1. Preheat broiler. Line broiler pan or baking sheet with foil. Place poblano peppers on foil; broil 5 to 6 inches from heat source 15 minutes or until peppers are blistered and beginning to char, turning occasionally. Place peppers in medium bowl; cover with plastic wrap. Let stand 20 minutes.

2. Meanwhile, heat oil in large saucepan over medium-high heat. Add onion, celery, carrots and garlic; cook and stir 4 minutes or until onion is translucent. Add broth; bring to a boil. Reduce heat to medium-low; cover and simmer 12 minutes or until celery is tender.

3. Remove skins, stems and seeds from peppers. Briefly run peppers under running water to help remove skins and seeds, if necessary. (This removes some smoky flavor, so work quickly.) Add peppers to broth mixture.

4. Working in batches, process broth mixture and cream cheese in food processor or blender until smooth; return to saucepan. Cook and stir over medium heat 2 minutes or until heated through. Season with salt and black pepper.

Curried Vegetable and Cashew Stew

Makes 6 servings

2 medium potatoes, peeled and cut into ½-inch cubes

12 ounces eggplant, cut into ½-inch cubes

1 can (about 15 ounces) chickpeas, rinsed and drained

1 medium onion, chopped

1 can (about 14 ounces) petite diced tomatoes

1 cup vegetable broth

2 tablespoons quick cooking tapioca

2 teaspoons grated fresh ginger

2 teaspoons curry powder

½ teaspoon salt

¼ teaspoon black pepper

1 medium zucchini (about 8 ounces), cut into ½-inch cubes

½ cup frozen peas

1 cup golden raisins

½ cup lightly salted cashews

Slow Cooker Directions

1. Combine potatoes, eggplant, chickpeas, onion, tomatoes, broth, tapioca, ginger, curry powder, salt and pepper in slow cooker. Cover; cook on LOW 8 to 9 hours.

2. Stir zucchini, peas, raisins and cashews into slow cooker. Turn slow cooker to HIGH. Cover; cook on HIGH 1 hour or until zucchini is tender.

A

B

C

Acknowledgments

The publisher would like to thank the companies and organizations listed below for the use of their recipes and photographs in this publication.

Campbell Soup Company
McCormick & Company, Inc.
National Turkey Federation
Ortega®, A Division of B&G Foods North America, Inc.
The Quaker® Oatmeal Kitchens
Sargento® Foods Inc.
© Sunbeam Products, Inc. doing business as Jarden Consumer Solutions.
US Dry Bean Council

Metric Conversion Chart

VOLUME MEASUREMENTS (dry)

$^1/_8$ teaspoon = 0.5 mL
$^1/_4$ teaspoon = 1 mL
$^1/_2$ teaspoon = 2 mL
$^3/_4$ teaspoon = 4 mL
1 teaspoon = 5 mL
1 tablespoon = 15 mL
2 tablespoons = 30 mL
$^1/_4$ cup = 60 mL
$^1/_3$ cup = 75 mL
$^1/_2$ cup = 125 mL
$^2/_3$ cup = 150 mL
$^3/_4$ cup = 175 mL
1 cup = 250 mL
2 cups = 1 pint = 500 mL
3 cups = 750 mL
4 cups = 1 quart = 1 L

VOLUME MEASUREMENTS (fluid)

1 fluid ounce (2 tablespoons) = 30 mL
4 fluid ounces ($^1/_2$ cup) = 125 mL
8 fluid ounces (1 cup) = 250 mL
12 fluid ounces (1$^1/_2$ cups) = 375 mL
16 fluid ounces (2 cups) = 500 mL

WEIGHTS (mass)

$^1/_2$ ounce = 15 g
1 ounce = 30 g
3 ounces = 90 g
4 ounces = 120 g
8 ounces = 225 g
10 ounces = 285 g
12 ounces = 360 g
16 ounces = 1 pound = 450 g

DIMENSIONS

$^1/_{16}$ inch = 2 mm
$^1/_8$ inch = 3 mm
$^1/_4$ inch = 6 mm
$^1/_2$ inch = 1.5 cm
$^3/_4$ inch = 2 cm
1 inch = 2.5 cm

OVEN TEMPERATURES

250°F = 120°C
275°F = 140°C
300°F = 150°C
325°F = 160°C
350°F = 180°C
375°F = 190°C
400°F = 200°C
425°F = 220°C
450°F = 230°C

BAKING PAN SIZES

Utensil	Size in Inches/Quarts	Metric Volume	Size in Centimeters
Baking or Cake Pan (square or rectangular)	8×8×2	2 L	20×20×5
	9×9×2	2.5 L	23×23×5
	12×8×2	3 L	30×20×5
	13×9×2	3.5 L	33×23×5
Loaf Pan	8×4×3	1.5 L	20×10×7
	9×5×3	2 L	23×13×7
Round Layer Cake Pan	8×1½	1.2 L	20×4
	9×1½	1.5 L	23×4
Pie Plate	8×1¼	750 mL	20×3
	9×1¼	1 L	23×3
Baking Dish or Casserole	1 quart	1 L	—
	1½ quart	1.5 L	—
	2 quart	2 L	—